MARK

FOR A NEW GENERATION

RYAN HELLER

MARK FOR A NEW GENERATION

© 2025 RYAN HELLER

Scripture quotations marked (CSB) have been taken from the Christian Standard Bible®, Copyright ©2017 by Holman Bible Publishers. Used by permission. Christian Standard Bible® and CSB® are federally registered trademarks of Holman Bible Publishers.

ISBN: 979-8-9996514-2-6 paperback
ISBN: 979-8-9996514-3-3 ebook

DEDICATION

To Zayne, Bryn, and your friends. Here is much of what you need to know about Jesus and the Gospel.

Getting Started

YOU'RE drowning, and someone tosses you a life preserver. You're starving, and someone sets a feast before you. You're wandering in darkness, and someone flips on the lights. That's what Jesus does throughout the Gospel of Mark. He shows up in people's desperate circumstances and provides exactly what they need.

Jesus offers something revolutionary and He actually delivers. When we read Mark from cover to cover, this truth becomes impossible to miss. Not just spiritual needs, but every human need imaginable.

And here's the beautiful part: We only begin to see the scope of Jesus' care when we experience Mark as the compelling story it was designed to be. No more skipping from verse to verse. No time for lightweight spirituality or filtered faith. We want the whole story, uncut.

Have you ever thought about how most people read Scripture? We treat it like museum patrons, lingering for a moment in front of each exhibit. We point out a miracle or two, we drop a teaching or two in conversation. But Mark's Gospel is not a museum. It's a raging river, and the torrent of Jesus' love is only revealed when we wade into the whole story. And when we do, we discover a Jesus who is attentive to our real needs in real time. The evidence of this is everywhere throughout Mark's story.

Think of the woman who'd been an outcast for twelve years. She spent her life hidden in the shadows until she touched a cloak in desperation and was changed forever. Imagine 5,000 hungry, nameless people on a hillside; no one to care for them, no one to see them. Jesus turned a boy's lunch into a banquet that left everyone full. Feel the fear of disciples in a boat being pounded by a storm they thought would kill them. Jesus spoke to the wind and the waves and brought them peace. See the demon-possessed man living among the tombs, rejected by society, half-naked and shattered. Jesus restored him whole.

The pages of Mark reveal this pattern over and over. Jesus meets physical needs through healing. He meets emotional needs through comfort. He meets spiritual needs through forgiveness. He meets practical needs through provision. Jesus touches lepers who need acceptance, gives sight to the blind who need vision, brings hope to those who are drowning in despair. Mark is revealing a rhythm of divine compassion responding to human need.

The truth that emerges from the story of Mark is this: the same Jesus who met needs two thousand years ago is still meeting needs today. The God who fed multitudes still provides. The Savior who calmed storms still brings peace to chaos. The Healer who restored broken bodies still mends broken lives. The pages of this book will reintroduce and reconnect a new generation to Jesus, proving Him to be the most relevant and powerful Being of all time.

As we read through Mark's Gospel in its entirety, something happens. We're not just reading ancient history. We're getting to know a Person. The more we know Jesus, the more we are certain of who He is and what He promises. Stress gives way to trust when we see His faithfulness revealed page after page. Power flows into our lives when we experience His authority over every circumstance. Clarity replaces confusion as His truth shines on our path.

This is Mark for a new generation—a generation weary of filtered faith and curated spirituality. You're ready for the real Jesus. The one who doesn't just inspire but transforms. Who doesn't just teach but rescues. Who doesn't just promise but delivers. His story is still being written, and the next chapter could be yours.

Ryan Heller

CONTENTS

1. The Best News You'll Ever Hear
~Mark 1:1-8~

The beginning of the gospel of Jesus Christ, the Son of God. As it is written in Isaiah the prophet: See, I am sending my messenger ahead of you; he will prepare your way. Mark 1:1-2 (CSB)

THE words tumbled out before Mark could stop himself. He had to tell this story, had to capture what it felt like when everything shifted. Not a lottery win or job promotion, but something that rewrote the fundamental operating system of existence itself. So he started with the only phrase that made sense: this is the beginning of the best news anyone will ever hear.

Mark doesn't call this "interesting news" or "important news." He calls it *gospel.* Good news. And that matters deeply. The Greek term "euangelion" was used to announce victories in battle or royal births. It carried weight because it meant something significant had shifted in favor of the people. When we examine our daily news consumption, how much actually improves our lives or fills us with hope? Most news leaves us feeling anxious, angry, or helpless.

But what's different about Mark's announcement is the good news doesn't depend on political outcomes, economic indicators, or cultural trends. It rests on the unshakeable reality of who Jesus is and what He accomplished. The good news Mark announces isn't temporary or conditional. It doesn't expire when circumstances change or feelings shift. This news remains good, whether we're celebrating victories or walking through valleys.

You know how some beginnings change everything? The first day of a new job. Meeting someone who becomes

1

important. The decision that redirects your entire path. Beginnings often feel small, but carry enormous power to reshape what follows. Mark emphasizes this is *the beginning* of good news, not the entirety. What he's about to tell us launches something that keeps expanding.

The beginning Mark describes isn't just historical. It's personal and immediate. When we truly encounter Jesus, we don't just learn about something from two thousand years ago. We step into our own beginning. Old patterns lose their grip. New possibilities emerge. Hope takes root where despair once dominated. THE good news about Jesus isn't information to file away for future reference. It's a new reality to inhabit daily.

This news transforms how we interpret setbacks, treat difficult people, respond to uncertainty. It provides a foundation that holds steady when everything else feels unstable.

Living in this good news means recognizing that our ultimate security doesn't depend on our performance, other people's approval, or favorable circumstances. The Son of God has entered human history and changed the fundamental equation of existence. We are known, loved, and secure in ways that transcend our immediate situations. This doesn't mean life becomes easy or problems disappear. But it does mean we have access to resources bigger than our challenges and hope more durable than our difficulties.

CALL TO ACTION #1: Start reading Mark today. Don't wait for the perfect time or ideal circumstances. Open to Mark 1:1 right now and read the first chapter. Let Jesus show you what He's really like.

CALL TO ACTION #2: Invite a friend who's struggling. Think of someone going through a tough time right now. Text them today and ask if they want to read Mark together. Let them discover the Jesus who meets real needs.

2. Level Up Spiritually
~Mark 1:9-11~

In those days Jesus came from Nazareth in Galilee and was baptized in the Jordan by John. As soon as he came up out of the water, he saw the heavens being torn open and the Spirit descending on him like a dove. Mark 1:9-10 (CSB)

LET'S be real. Nowadays, everyone is going public about something. Engagements, business launches, gym progress, even what they had for lunch. But there's a question that cuts deeper: Have you gone public with your faith?

If anyone could have skipped baptism, it was Jesus. Perfect. Sinless. Already one with God. Yet He chose to step into the muddy waters of the Jordan. Why? Because baptism isn't just a ritual; it's a declaration, an alignment, and an activation.

Yet here we are in a world that has changed so much since then. Many people question, does baptism still matter? If so, why?

Decision – Going Public with Your Faith

JESUS didn't keep His commitment to God private. He made it known—out loud, out front, in the open.

Baptism is your chance to make your faith official. It's a visible moment where you say, "This is who I am now. I follow Jesus."

Remember the Ethiopian eunuch in Acts 8? The moment he saw water, he said, "What's stopping me from being baptized?" The urgency was real.

Association – Identifying with Jesus

ROMANS 6:3-5 says baptism links us to Jesus' death and resurrection. When you go under, you're burying your old self. When you come up, you're walking into a brand-new life. Jesus didn't need that transformation, but He chose to stand with us. Through baptism, we stand with Him.

Authorization – Empowered for God's Mission

RIGHT after His baptism, Jesus was launched into His mission. He didn't go back to life as usual; He stepped into His calling.

Baptism isn't the finish line; it's your starting gate. It's God's way of saying, "You're ready. Let's go."

"You are my beloved Son; with you I am well-pleased" (Mark 1:11). That's not just for Jesus. When you're baptized, you step into that same affirmation. You are God's beloved. You carry His approval, His Spirit, and His purpose.

CALL TO ACTION #1: Change your relationship status with Jesus from "it's complicated" to "committed." Step into your next chapter. If you've trusted Jesus but haven't been baptized, what's holding you back? This week, reach out to your pastor or church. Don't wait. Make it official. Go public.

CALL TO ACTION #2: You've got God's blue checkmark—now start posting like it. Serve like you're on a mission...because you are. Already baptized? Ask yourself, "Am I living like someone who's been authorized by God?" This week, choose one bold action that reflects your calling. Show up. Speak out.

3. Shocking Truth About Discipleship
~Mark 1:12-13~

Immediately the Spirit drove him into the wilderness. He was in the wilderness forty days, being tempted by Satan. He was with the wild animals, and the angels were serving him. Mark 1:12-13 (CSB)

NOBODY tells you that spiritual mountaintops often lead straight into spiritual battles. Jesus had just experienced a mountaintop moment: heaven opened, the Spirit descended, the Father's voice declared His love.

And then? *Immediately the Spirit drove him into the wilderness.* Not gently led. Not gradually guided. Drove. The same Spirit that blessed Him launched Him into hardship, a desolate place where He experienced intense temptation.

You're Not Alone in the Fight

THE Reality Check: You will be tempted the most when you're trying the hardest to follow God. That promotion at work might bring new ethical challenges. That decision to get serious about your faith might trigger unexpected opposition. That commitment to purity might intensify the battle against lust.

But this is the game-changer: Jesus has already walked this road. He faced Satan head-on for forty days, not as a show of power, but as a statement of solidarity with you.

Wild Animals and Angels

MARK includes a detail the other Gospel writers left out: Jesus was *with the wild animals*. Picture it: lions, bears,

5

whatever predators roamed that wilderness. Yet He survived. Why? Because *the angels were serving him.*

When you're in your wilderness (facing temptation, spiritual attack, or overwhelming circumstances), God doesn't abandon you there. He strengthens you there. Angels are ministering spirits sent to help believers. That unexpected encouragement, that sense someone was praying for you, that supernatural peace in the storm— God's supernatural provision is real.

Jesus didn't stay in the wilderness. After forty days, He emerged victorious and ready for ministry. Your desert season has an expiration date. God isn't punishing you… He's preparing you.

CALL TO ACTION #1: Don't white-knuckle your way through temptation when you can phone a friend who's never lost. When you face temptation or spiritual attack, remember that Jesus understands. He faced the same enemy and won. What temptation are you facing right now? Turn to Jesus for strength and victory.

CALL TO ACTION #2: God has angels on your payroll and you didn't even know it—say thanks to the invisible workforce. Angels are ministering spirits sent to help believers. Take time today to thank God for His supernatural protection and provision in your life, even when you can't see it.

4. Time For A Turnaround
~Mark 1:14-15~

After John was arrested, Jesus went to Galilee, proclaiming the good news of God: "The time is fulfilled, and the kingdom of God has come near. Repent and believe the good news!" Mark 1:14-15 (CSB)

WHAT if I told you that the most life-changing conversation you could have with God starts with admitting you've been going the wrong direction? Most people think repentance is about feeling bad about your mistakes. But Jesus reveals something far more powerful in His very first sermon.

The Perfect Timing

NOTICE the context: John the Baptist had just been arrested—his ministry cut short, his voice silenced. But instead of retreating, Jesus stepped forward with an urgent message. *"The time is fulfilled, and the kingdom of God has come near."*

This wasn't random timing. Jesus was announcing that everything the prophets had predicted, everything God had promised, everything humanity had been waiting for was finally happening. The moment had arrived. God's kingdom wasn't coming someday. It was arriving right then, right there. And the entry requirement wasn't perfection or religious performance. It was a complete turnaround.

The Gospel in Two Words

JESUS distilled the entire gospel message into two powerful commands: *"Repent and believe the good news!"* This isn't just Mark's summary; this is the gospel.

Repent doesn't mean feeling sorry and promising to try harder. The Greek word "metanoia" means to change your mind completely, to do a 180-degree turn. It's recognizing that your way isn't working and choosing God's way instead.

Believe the good news means trusting that Christ was crucified for your sins and raised for your victory. It's not just intellectual agreement, it's staking your life on the truth that Jesus has done what you could never do.

More Than Sorry

MOST people get stuck confusing regret with repentance. Regret says, "I feel bad about what I did." Repentance says, "I'm changing direction completely." Regret focuses on the past; repentance focuses on the future.

True repentance sees your sin from God's perspective, makes the hard decision to cut it off completely, and asks the Holy Spirit for the power to break free. It's not about managing your sin; it's about experiencing total transformation.

Repentance isn't a one-time event; it's a lifestyle. Every day, we discover new areas where we need to turn from our way and embrace God's way. It's the ongoing process of aligning our lives with His kingdom values.

The Kingdom Is Near

THE most encouraging part of Jesus' message? *The kingdom of God has come near.* You don't have to wait until you get your act together. You don't have to earn your way in. The moment you repent and believe, you step into God's kingdom reality.

The kingdom isn't just about heaven someday; it's about experiencing God's rule and reign in your life today. It's about living with His power, His peace, His purpose, and His presence right now.

The Urgency of Now

JESUS said, *"The time is fulfilled."* There's an urgency to His message that we can't ignore. The opportunity to respond to God's grace is available now, but it won't be available forever. Every day you delay is a day you miss out on the abundant life God wants to give you.

The kingdom of God isn't waiting for you to get perfect; it's waiting for you to get honest. It's waiting for you to admit that your way isn't working and that you need a Savior.

CALL TO ACTION #1: Acknowledge that your way isn't working. Pinpoint one specific area where you're going in the wrong direction, whether it's in your relationships, mindset, habits, or priorities. Name it. Turn from it. Ask God for a complete shift, not just temporary regret.

CALL TO ACTION #2: Don't delay your response to God's invitation. Jesus said, *"The time is fulfilled."* That means the window of opportunity is open right now. Every time you say, "I'll deal with it later," your heart grows a little colder and your excuses get a little louder. Take action today and step into God's kingdom.

5. What Are You Waiting For?
~Mark 1:16-20~

"Follow me," Jesus told them, "and I will make you fish for people."
Immediately they left their nets and followed him.
Mark 1:17-18 (CSB)

IT IS now common for people to ghost their dates, quit jobs via text, and need three business days to respond to a simple message. But imagine dropping everything (your career, your family business, your entire five-year plan) because someone you just met said: "Follow me." That's exactly what happened when Jesus called His first disciples.

No Hesitation, No Negotiation

NOTICE what these men didn't do. They didn't say, "Let me pray about it." They didn't ask for a detailed ministry plan or request references from Jesus' previous disciples. They didn't negotiate terms or ask about salary and benefits. They heard the call and responded immediately.

Simon, Andrew, James, and John were successful fishermen with established businesses. They had responsibilities, employees, and family obligations. Yet when Jesus extended His invitation, they abandoned their nets without a second thought. Their response wasn't reckless, it was radical obedience.

The Cost of Waiting

IN our environment of endless deliberation, we've turned decision-making into an art form of procrastination. We analyze, strategize, and theorize until the moment passes us by. But immediate obedience to God's call isn't about making hasty decisions; it's about recognizing divine opportunity when it presents itself.

The disciples understood something we often miss: some invitations from God come with expiration dates. The fishing boats would still be there tomorrow, but this moment with Jesus might not be. They recognized that following Christ wasn't just another life choice; it was *the* life choice that would define everything else.

Beyond Comfort Zones

THESE fishermen didn't just leave their profession; they left their comfort zone. Fishing was what they knew, what they were good at, what provided security. Jesus was calling them into the unknown, promising to make them "fishers of people"—a job description they couldn't fully comprehend.

God's calls often require us to step beyond our expertise and into His sufficiency. He doesn't always provide a detailed roadmap because He wants us to trust Him step by step. The disciples' immediate response demonstrated faith in Jesus' character, not just His plan.

Do Not Delay

SCRIPTURE repeatedly emphasizes the importance of responding to God's voice without delay. Hebrews 3:15 warns: *Today, if you hear his voice, do not harden your hearts.* The word *today* appears over 300 times in the Bible, underscoring God's emphasis on present-moment obedience.

What is God calling you to do that you've been putting off? Maybe it's having that difficult conversation, taking that step of faith, or making that commitment you've been avoiding. Perhaps He's calling you to serve in a new capacity, pursue a different direction, or simply trust Him with a current struggle.

RYAN HELLER

The Promise in the Call

JESUS didn't just call the disciples away from something; He called them toward something greater. *"I will make you fish for people"* wasn't just a career change; it was a destiny upgrade. When we respond immediately to God's call, we position ourselves to receive His transformation and training.

The same Jesus who called fishermen to become world-changers is calling you today. He sees potential in you that you might not even recognize. But His ability to develop that potential often depends on your willingness to respond without delay.

CALL TO ACTION #1: Identify and obey. Stop making excuses and start making moves. Right now, identify one specific area where you know God has been calling you to act. Write it down, pray about it, and then take the first concrete step today—not tomorrow, not next week, but today.

CALL TO ACTION #2: Abandon your nets. Release what's holding you back and embrace what God is calling you toward. What "nets" in your life represent security, comfort, or familiarity that might be preventing you from following Jesus more fully? Make the decision to let go and trust Him with your future.

The disciples' immediate response changed not only their lives but the entire world. What might God do through your immediate obedience? There's only one way to find out. What are you waiting for?

6. When Evil Meets Its Match
~Mark 1:21-28~

They were astonished at his teaching because he was teaching them as one who had authority, and not like the scribes. Just then a man with an unclean spirit was in their synagogue. Mark 1:21-23 (CSB)

IMAGINE you are walking into a room and the second you set foot in the doorway, your worst enemy begins screaming your name and begging for mercy. This was the scene when Jesus walked into a synagogue in Capernaum. The religious crowd was in the midst of trying to discern who this new teacher was, but the demons knew…and they were afraid.

The people were amazed at Jesus' teaching because He taught *as one who had authority, and not like the scribes.* But it wasn't just His teaching that had this power, His very presence put the demons on edge. The demonic spirit could no longer stay hidden or silent when Jesus was in town. Spiritual opposition will follow you as soon as you start doing God's will seriously. You could call it a spiritual attack, but know this: it didn't faze Jesus.

There are two very dangerous positions that people take with the demonic. Some never think about demonic activity at all; it's just not in their equations. Other people see demons around every corner and attribute any inconvenience in their lives to spiritual warfare. If your car won't start, you probably just need a new battery, not deliverance.

The truth is in the middle: spiritual warfare is real, but so is Jesus' complete authority over it. We should never get to the place where we stop allowing space to understand the demonic realm in our lives, but we should always remember that Jesus has already won.

The good news is that Jesus has given us authority over demonic activity. When a young boy in our church was hearing voices that told him to hurt himself, prayer in the name of Jesus brought total freedom. That night he slept soundly with the lights off and never heard those voices again. It is scary. It is intimidating. But the power of Jesus is greater than any spiritual attack you will face.

CALL TO ACTION #1: Stand on your authority. Use the name of Jesus instead of fighting spiritual battles in your own strength. If you are in a place of spiritual oppression or attack, identify any area where you feel like there is spiritual resistance in your life and take authority over it through prayer in Jesus' name.

CALL TO ACTION #2: Draw on Jesus' power. When you are tempted or being spiritually attacked, remember that Jesus understands. He faced the same enemy and won. What temptation are you facing right now? Turn to Jesus for strength and victory instead of white-knuckling your way through it.

7. Jesus' Touch
~Mark 1:29-34~

As soon as they left the synagogue, they went into Simon and Andrew's house with James and John. Simon's mother-in-law was lying in bed with a fever, and they told him about her at once. So he went to her, took her by the hand, and raised her up. The fever left her, and she began to serve them. Mark 1:29-31 (CSB)

IN our swipe-right, DM-sliding, emoji-reacting world, we've forgotten the power of actual human touch. We can "connect" with hundreds of people without ever making real contact. But Jesus understood something we've lost: sometimes the most powerful thing you can do is simply reach out and touch someone.

Jesus Wasn't Afraid to Touch

SIMON'S mother-in-law had a fever. She was sick, possibly contagious, definitely not someone most people would want to get close to. But Jesus didn't hesitate. *He took her by the hand, and raised her up.* Throughout the Gospels, Jesus touches lepers, blind people, and the demon-possessed. He wasn't afraid of physical contact with hurting people.

There's something powerful about physical touch, just reaching your hand out and touching somebody. Jesus was never afraid to do that. He cares and He touches.

Touch That Transforms

NOTICE what happened after Jesus healed Peter's mother-in-law: *The fever left her, and she began to serve them.* When Jesus touches your life, the most natural response is to start serving others. It's not forced or guilt-driven. It's the natural outcome of experiencing His healing power.

That's why it's concerning when Christians want to be born again but don't want to exhibit life-change. When you truly encounter Jesus, you want to tell everybody about Him and serve others.

A House Full of Healing

WORD spread quickly. By evening, *they brought to him all those who were sick and demon-possessed. The whole town was assembled at the door, and he healed many who were sick with various diseases and drove out many demons (Mark 1:32-34)*. One touch led to a neighborhood transformation.

Jesus' willingness to get involved in someone's mess— to literally reach out and touch the untouchable—created a ripple effect that reached an entire community.

CALL TO ACTION #1: Stop being a digital bystander and start being an IRL (in real life) difference-maker. Jesus wasn't afraid to touch the sick and hurting. Who in your life needs the healing touch of Jesus through you? It might be a literal touch of comfort, or it might be reaching out with practical help. Don't be afraid to get involved in someone's mess this week.

CALL TO ACTION #2: Access the ultimate healing specialist instead of trying to diagnose yourself. Time to get off the couch and into the action. Notice that after being healed, Peter's mother-in-law immediately began serving. When Jesus touches your life, service becomes natural. How are you serving others as a response to what Jesus has done for you? If you're not serving anywhere, find a place to get involved this week.

8. The Secret To Spiritual Power
~Mark 1:35-38~

Very early in the morning, while it was still dark, he got up, went out, and made his way to a deserted place. And there he was praying.
Mark 1:35 (CSB)

EVER feel like your day starts with chaos before your feet even hit the floor? Notifications, texts, screaming headlines, and endless to-do lists. It's like the world is shouting at you before you've had a chance to think.

But Jesus shows us another way. Before the noise, He sought the quiet. Before the demands, He embraced the divine. If the Son of God needed solitude with the Father to walk in power, how much more do we?

Jesus was on mission in Galilee—teaching, healing, and confronting darkness. Yet, before any of that, He withdrew. Why? Because He knew His strength came not from the crowds, but from His connection with the Father. And if we want to live with spiritual power, we must follow His example.

Mark 1 gives us a simple but profound rhythm to build into our devotional lives:

Pick a Place

JESUS went to a *deserted place*. Not just anywhere. A specific, quiet place where He could be alone. You need your own sacred space too, whether it's a corner of your living room, your parked car, a walk around the block, or a comfy chair by a window. Make it your place with God.

The location doesn't have to be perfect or Instagram-worthy. It just needs to be consistent and free from distractions. Jesus chose a deserted place because He needed to get away from the demands and expectations of others. You need the same kind of space where you can be honest with God without performance or pretense.

Set a Time

JESUS prayed early in the morning. There's power in meeting with God before you meet with the world. Morning isn't a rule, but it is a powerful rhythm. When you start your day with God, you set the tone for everything that follows.

Whenever you choose (morning, midday, or night), consistency is key. Pick a time and protect it like an appointment with your closest friend. Your relationship with God deserves the same priority you give to important meetings or commitments.

Avoid Distractions

"EVERYONE is looking for you," the disciples told Jesus in Mark 1:37. Still, He stayed focused. Jesus didn't allow the urgent to divert His attention from the important. Neither should we. Your inbox can wait. Your kids, your coworkers, your calendar—none of them need you more than you need Him.

This is where most people fail in their prayer life. They start with good intentions, but then allow interruptions to derail their time with God. Protect your prayer time like you would protect any other important appointment.

Expect God to Move

AFTER praying, in Mark 1:39 Jesus went out preaching and casting out demons. There's a pattern here: prayer before power. If we want to see God move in our lives, we need to spend time with Him. Prayer doesn't just prepare us, it empowers us.

Jesus didn't pray just to check a box or fulfill a religious obligation. He prayed because He knew that His ministry effectiveness depended on His connection with the Father. The same is true for us. When we prioritize prayer, we position ourselves to experience God's power in our daily lives.

The Power Connection

THE secret to spiritual power isn't complicated; it's consistent communion with God. Jesus modeled this rhythm because He knew that everything He needed for life and ministry flowed from His relationship with the Father.

CALL TO ACTION #1: Reset your rhythm. This week, choose a consistent time and place to meet with God. Start with just 10-15 minutes a day. Write it on your calendar. Set a reminder. Make it sacred. When you prioritize prayer, you position yourself for power.

CALL TO ACTION #2: Pray with purpose. Replace lottery-style prayers with focused, intentional communication. Identify one area of your life where you desperately need God's power—maybe it's a relationship, a decision, or an emotional struggle. Commit to pray specifically about that one thing every day this week. Watch what happens when you align your heart with His.

9. Jesus Touches The Untouchable
~Mark 1:39-45~

Then a man with leprosy came to him and, on his knees, begged him, "If you are willing, you can make me clean." Moved with compassion, Jesus reached out his hand and touched him. "I am willing," he told him. "Be made clean." Mark 1:40–41 (CSB)

WE live in a culture quick to cancel, unfollow, and push away what's uncomfortable or broken. But Jesus? He moves toward the mess. While everyone else keeps their distance from the broken, He reaches out to embrace them.

Jesus is gaining momentum in His ministry—preaching, healing, and casting out demons across Galilee. The spiritual battle is real, and it's intensifying. But then comes a deeply human, personal moment that cuts through all the chaos: a man with leprosy kneels before Jesus and says, *"If you are willing, you can make me clean."*

The Utmost Outcast

LEPROSY wasn't just a physical disease, it was a social and spiritual exile. These men and women were cast out of towns, cut off from community, and declared unclean by law. No one would touch them. Most wouldn't even make eye contact.

Imagine living in complete isolation, watching your body deteriorate while your relationships disintegrate. Imagine being forced to shout, "Unclean! Unclean!" whenever anyone approached, warning them to stay away from your contamination. Imagine years without human touch, without community, without hope.

That was this man's reality. Yet somehow, he heard about Jesus. Maybe word had spread about this teacher who welcomed sinners, who ate with tax collectors, who didn't seem to follow the normal rules about who was acceptable and who wasn't.

The Risky Approach

THE man's approach was incredibly risky. By coming to Jesus, he was breaking social protocol and religious law. He was supposed to stay isolated, not approach a rabbi in public. But desperation drove him past propriety.

His words reveal both faith and uncertainty: *"If you are willing, you can make me clean."* He believed Jesus had the power. That wasn't the question. The question was whether Jesus would choose to use that power for someone like him.

The Revolutionary Touch

BUT Jesus did more than look at the man with leprosy. He touched him. In doing so, Jesus broke religious traditions, risked His reputation, and shattered societal expectations. But His compassion was greater than the cost.

This wasn't just healing, it was restoration. The touch came before the cure. Jesus didn't heal him first and then touch him when it was safe. He touched him while he was still unclean, still contagious, still untouchable.

That touch communicated something profound: "You're not too far gone. You're not too broken. You're not disqualified from love." Before the man's body was healed, his dignity was restored.

The Willing Savior

JESUS' response was immediate and definitive: *"I am willing. Be made clean."* No hesitation. No conditions. No requirements for the man to prove himself worthy first.

The same Jesus who touched the leper is still willing today. He's still reaching toward the broken, the isolated, the ones who feel too contaminated for grace. He's still saying, *"I am willing,"* to anyone brave enough to approach Him with their need.

The Heart of Jesus

THAT'S who Jesus is. He's not afraid of brokenness; He steps into it. He's not bound by tradition; He's driven by love. He doesn't just heal bodies; He restores dignity. And today, He's still reaching for those who feel too far gone.

CALL TO ACTION #1: Cross the line of comfort and reach out to people others avoid. Who in your life is easy to dismiss or distance yourself from? Maybe it's someone difficult, different, or just in pain. This week, ask Jesus to help you move beyond your comfort zone and reach out through a conversation, a kind gesture, or simply by being present.

CALL TO ACTION #2: Accept God's unlimited warranty on forgiveness instead of disqualifying yourself from His grace. The man said, *"If you are willing."* Maybe you're wondering the same. Is Jesus willing to heal you? To restore your broken places? The answer is still the same: "I am willing." Come to Him with your pain. Trust Him with your need. He's not just able, He's eager to make you whole.

10. Friends and Faith
~Mark 2:1-12~

When he entered Capernaum again after some days, it was reported that he was at home. So many people gathered together that there was no more room, not even in the doorway, and he was speaking the word to them. They came to him bringing a paralytic, carried by four of them. Mark 2:1-4 (CSB)

IN life, you're going to face moments when you can't walk on your own physically, emotionally, or spiritually. The real question is, who's on your roof team?

Who will carry you when you're down and break through barriers to get you to Jesus? Even more importantly, who are you doing that for?

The Impossible Situation

JESUS is back in Capernaum. Word spreads, and soon the house He's teaching in is standing-room only. Enter four men carrying their paralyzed friend. They get to the house and hit a wall. Literally. No room inside. No way through the crowd.

Most people would have given up at this point. "Well, we tried. Maybe next time." But these four friends weren't most people. They had carried their friend this far, and they weren't about to let a crowded room defeat them.

The Faith That Moved Jesus

THIS is the moment that changes everything: *"Seeing their faith..." (Mark 2:5).* Not the paralytic's faith. It was the faith of his friends that caught Jesus' attention and moved Him to act. That's intercession. That's spiritual friendship. That's what we're called to.

The four men believed so strongly that Jesus could heal their friend that they were willing to tear up someone's roof to make it happen. Their faith was active, persistent, and sacrificial. They didn't just pray for their friend; they carried him. They didn't just hope for a miracle; they created an opportunity for one.

The Power of Spiritual Friendship

THESE were "whatever-it-takes" friends—the kind we all need and the kind we're called to be. Friends who don't just talk about Jesus, but actually bring people to Him through prayer, boldness, and persistence.

The paralyzed man couldn't get to Jesus on his own. He needed friends who would carry him when he couldn't walk, who would fight for him when he couldn't fight, who would believe for him when his own faith might have been weak.

The Modern Roof-Rippers

YOU don't have to tear up a roof today, but maybe you need to tear through your comfort zone, fear of rejection, or your packed schedule. Someone around you may be paralyzed by anxiety, addiction, depression, or doubt. Your faith could be the bridge that brings them to healing.

Maybe it's inviting them to church when you know they might say no. Maybe it's having that difficult conversation about faith. Maybe it's consistently praying for them even when you don't see results. Maybe it's simply being present in their pain and pointing them toward hope.

The Faith That Carries Others

THE beautiful truth is that Jesus still responds to the faith of friends. When you intercede for someone, when you carry them in prayer, when you refuse to give up on them, Jesus sees that faith. Your persistence matters. Your prayers count. Your love makes a difference.

CALL TO ACTION #1: Be a roof-ripper. Who in your life needs help getting to Jesus? Don't let obstacles, excuses, or discomfort prevent you from acting. Reach out, pray for them, invite them to church or a small group. Do something bold this week to help them encounter Christ.

CALL TO ACTION #2: Become a spiritual first responder instead of a prayer tourist. Jesus responded to the faith of friends. Who are you interceding for right now? If you're not sure, ask God to highlight someone. Then commit to pray daily for their salvation, healing, or breakthrough. Your faith may unlock their miracle.

11. Crash The Party
~Mark 2:13-17~

"It is not those who are well who need a doctor, but those who are sick. I didn't come to call the righteous, but sinners." Mark 2:17 (CSB)

THE best parties always have the most interesting guest lists, and Jesus threw the most controversial dinner party in history—one that changed everything.

In Mark 2:13-17, we meet Levi (also known as Matthew), a wealthy tax collector who was basically the ancient equivalent of a corrupt politician. These guys were despised—they got rich by overcharging their own people and pocketing the difference. Yet when Jesus simply said, "Follow me," Levi immediately left his lucrative scam behind.

But this is where it gets good: Levi's first move as a new believer? He threw a massive party and invited all his shady friends to meet Jesus. Evangelism with style!

The Immediate Response

WHAT strikes me about Levi's story is the immediacy of his response. Jesus called, and Levi *got up and followed him (Mark 2:14)*. No hesitation. No negotiation. No "let me think about it." He walked away from a profitable career to follow an itinerant preacher with no guaranteed income.

This wasn't just a career change, it was complete life transformation. Tax collectors were social outcasts, hated by their own people for collaborating with Rome. But Levi saw something in Jesus that was worth more than money, more valuable than security, more important than reputation.

The Party Strategy

LEVI'S first instinct as a new follower wasn't to distance himself from his old life, it was to introduce his old friends to his new Lord. He threw a party and invited *many tax collectors and sinners* to meet Jesus *(Mark 2:15)*.

This is brilliant evangelism. Levi knew his friends wouldn't come to a synagogue or respond to street preaching. But they would come to a party. He created a comfortable environment where his friends could encounter Jesus naturally, without pressure or pretense.

The Religious Police

THE Pharisees were horrified. *"Why does he eat with tax collectors and sinners?"* they demanded *(Mark 2:16)*. Their question revealed their fundamental misunderstanding of Jesus' mission.

In their minds, holy people stayed away from unholy people to avoid contamination. They believed righteousness was about separation, not transformation. They thought God's love was earned through good behavior, not freely given to the broken.

The Doctor's Diagnosis

JESUS' response was brilliant: *"It is not those who are well who need a doctor, but those who are sick. I didn't come to call the righteous, but sinners."*

This wasn't Jesus endorsing sin, it was Jesus explaining His mission. He came to heal the spiritually sick, not to congratulate the spiritually healthy. The problem was that the Pharisees thought they were healthy when they were actually the sickest of all.

If you think you're spiritually healthy, you probably don't think you need Jesus. But if you know you're broken, congratulations, you're exactly who Jesus came for.

The Beautiful Truth

THE beautiful truth of this story is that Jesus doesn't wait for us to clean up our act before He calls us. He calls us in our mess and then helps us clean up. He doesn't love us because we're good; He loves us because He's good.

Levi didn't have to quit being a tax collector before Jesus called him. Jesus called him as a tax collector and then transformed him into a disciple. The same grace that reached Levi reaches us today.

The Ongoing Mission

JESUS is still crashing parties, still eating with sinners, still calling the broken and the lost. The question is, are we creating opportunities for our friends to meet Him? Are we building bridges or walls between the lost and the Savior?

CALL TO ACTION #1: Invite someone over. Like Matthew, when we encounter Christ, we should want to share Him with others. Who are the "tax collectors and sinners" in your life that you could invite to hear about Jesus? Don't be afraid to associate with people who need the good news. Create opportunities for your friends to encounter Jesus in comfortable, natural settings.

CALL TO ACTION #2: Embrace your need for the doctor. Jesus came for the sick, not the healthy. The Great Physician specializes in cases that seem hopeless. Remember, Jesus didn't come for people who have it all together. He came for people like us—beautifully broken and desperately in need of grace.

12. Cable Couldn't Keep Up
~Mark 2:18-22~

And no one puts new wine into old wineskins. Otherwise, the wine will burst the skins, and the wine is lost as well as the skins. No, new wine is put into fresh wineskins. Mark 2:22 (CSB)

REMEMBER when cable companies tried to compete with Netflix by just adding "on demand" features? Epic fail. You can't put revolutionary technology into an outdated business model, and Jesus knew this better than anyone.

The Fasting Police Strike Again

IN Mark 2:18-22, the religious leaders were puzzled: *"Why do John's disciples and the Pharisees' disciples fast, but your disciples do not fast?"* They expected Jesus to follow their traditional playbook of somber religious rituals.

Jesus dropped three game-changing illustrations that basically said, "You're missing the point entirely."

Wedding Guests Don't Diet

FIRST, Jesus asked: *"The wedding guests cannot fast while the groom is with them, can they?" (Mark 2:19)*. In other words, "I'm here! This is celebration time, not mourning time!" When the Son of God shows up, you don't fast; you feast. Jesus' presence should bring joy, not just religious duty.

The religious leaders were stuck in funeral mode while Jesus was throwing a wedding party. They couldn't understand why His followers seemed so happy. But Jesus wasn't offering minor improvements to their existing religious system. He was announcing something completely new.

New Wine, New Wineskins

THEN Jesus got practical: *"No one puts new wine into old wineskins. Otherwise, the wine will burst the skins, and the wine is lost as well as the skins. No, new wine is put into fresh wineskins."*

In Jesus' time, wine was stored in animal skins that would stretch as the wine fermented. Old wineskins had already been stretched to their limit and would burst if you put fresh, fermenting wine in them. New wine needed new, flexible containers that could handle the expansion.

Jesus wasn't offering a patch job on old religion. He was bringing a completely new covenant. The joy, freedom, and power of the gospel can't be contained in rigid religious systems. You can't download grace 2.0 onto legalism 1.0.

The Cable Problem

THIS is exactly what happened to cable TV. They tried to adapt streaming innovation to their existing model instead of recognizing that the entire game had changed. They added on-demand features but couldn't let go of contracts, commercials, and rigid schedules.

The religious leaders had the same problem. They wanted Jesus' power and popularity, but they weren't willing to abandon their system of rules and religious performance. They wanted to add Jesus to their existing program instead of letting Him transform everything.

The Joy Revolution

WHAT Jesus brought wasn't just a new set of rules. It was a completely different relationship with God. Instead of earning God's approval through religious performance, people could receive it as a gift through faith. Instead of

30

fear-based compliance, they could experience love-based transformation.

This new wine of grace was too powerful for the old wineskins of legalism. It required a completely new approach to spirituality; one based on relationship rather than rules, joy rather than duty, grace rather than performance.

The religious leaders missed this because they were more committed to their methods than their mission. They valued their traditions more than transformation. They preferred the predictability of old wineskins to the adventure of new wine.

CALL TO ACTION #1: Audit your "wineskins." Jesus brings new life that can't be contained in old religious forms. What outdated religious habits or traditions might be limiting your experience of God's grace? Ask God to show you where you need "new wineskins" in your spiritual life, fresh ways of thinking and living that can actually contain His transforming power.

CALL TO ACTION #2: Choose joy over duty. Jesus' presence should bring celebration, not just obligation. How can you express joy in your relationship with Christ today instead of just going through religious motions? Find one specific way to celebrate what Jesus has done for you rather than treating faith like a checklist.

Christianity isn't Judaism with Jesus added. It's a completely new relationship with God based on grace through faith. Don't let old wineskins burst under the pressure of new wine.

13. When Karen Calls
~Mark 2:23-27~

On the Sabbath he was going through the grainfields, and his disciples began to make their way, picking some heads of grain. The Pharisees said to him, "Look, why are they doing what is not lawful on the Sabbath?" Mark 2:23-24 (CSB)

EVERYBODY has come across *that* person—the one who calls the cops on kids selling lemonade without a permit. Well, the Pharisees were the original Karens, and they just spotted Jesus' disciples breaking their precious rules.

The Sabbath Police Strike Again

IN Mark 2:23-24, Jesus and His disciples were walking through grain fields on the Sabbath when hunger struck. The disciples did what anyone would do: They grabbed some grain to snack on. Perfectly legal, totally normal.

But the Pharisees were watching, clipboard in hand: *"Look, why are they doing what is not lawful on the Sabbath?"* These religious rule-enforcers had turned God's gift of rest into a 39-category list of "don't do this." Picking grain? That's harvesting. Harvesting is work. Work is forbidden. Case closed... or so they thought.

Jesus Drops the Mic

JESUS didn't argue their technicalities. Instead, He reminded them of David, who ate sacred bread when he was hungry (1 Samuel 21). Then came the game-changer. *"The Sabbath was made for man and not man for the Sabbath. So then, the Son of Man is Lord even of the Sabbath"* (Mark 2:27-28).

In other words, "You've got this completely backwards. God didn't create people to serve rules. He created rules to serve people. And by the way, I'm the one with authority here."

The Heart Behind the Rule

GOD designed the Sabbath as a gift, not a burden. It was meant to provide rest, restoration, and refocus—not create anxiety about what you can and can't do. The Pharisees had weaponized worship and turned blessing into bondage.

CALL TO ACTION #1: Stop treating faith like a spiritual fitness tracker. God cares about your heart, not your streak. Are you treating God's gifts (like rest, worship, prayer, or Bible reading) as burdens or blessings? Ask God to reveal where you might be more focused on religious performance than on relationship with Him. Remember, Jesus came to give life, not more rules to stress about.

CALL TO ACTION #2: Trade your spiritual anxiety for Jesus-approved rest. Jesus declared Himself Lord of the Sabbath, meaning He has authority over how you rest, worship, and recharge. What does healthy spiritual rhythm look like in your life? Don't let legalistic thinking rob you of the joy and refreshment God intended. Let Jesus define what true rest looks like for you.

Remember, religion says, "Follow the rules perfectly." Jesus says, "Follow me and find rest for your soul." Choose relationship over rule-keeping every time.

14. Sabbath Sabotage
~Mark 3:1-6~

After looking around at them with anger, he was grieved at the hardness of their hearts and told the man, "Stretch out your hand." So he stretched it out, and his hand was restored. Immediately the Pharisees went out and started plotting with the Herodians against him, how they might kill him. Mark 3:5-6 (CSB)

YOU post a video of yourself helping someone in need, only to have the comment section explode with people criticizing you for doing it "wrong." Welcome to Jesus' life, where even healing someone got Him canceled.

The Setup: Compassion vs. Compliance

IN Mark 3:1-6, Jesus walked into a synagogue where a man with a withered hand was present. But this wasn't just a worship service; it was a trap. The religious leaders weren't concerned about the man's suffering; they were watching Jesus like hawks, hoping to catch Him breaking their Sabbath rules. *"In order to accuse him, they were watching him closely to see whether he would heal him on the Sabbath" (Mark 3:2).*

Talk about twisted priorities. A man needed healing, but all they cared about was their religious reputation.

Jesus Calls Them Out

JESUS didn't sneak around their rules. He confronted their heartlessness head-on. He told the man to stand up in front of everyone, then asked the crowd: *"Is it lawful to do good on the Sabbath or to do evil, to save life or to kill?" (Mark 3:4).*

Crickets. They had no answer because their hearts were harder than concrete.

Jesus became angry, not at the man's condition but at their callous indifference. Then He said, *"Stretch out your hand."* The man obeyed, and his hand was completely restored.

The Plot Twist Nobody Saw Coming

YOU'D think everyone would celebrate, right? Wrong. The religious leaders *immediately went out and started plotting with the Herodians against him, how they might kill him.*

They were so obsessed with their rules that they wanted to murder the One who came to save them. Religious tradition without love had become deadly.

CALL TO ACTION #1: Choose people over performance. Jesus was angry at religious leaders who cared more about rules than people's suffering. Examine your own heart. Are there areas where you've become more concerned with religious correctness than showing love and compassion? Ask God to reveal where you might be prioritizing appearance over authentic care for others.

CALL TO ACTION #2: Stretch out your brokenness. The man with the withered hand had to stretch out his hand in faith before Jesus healed him. What area of brokenness in your life do you need to stretch out to Jesus in faith today? Stop hiding your struggles and boldly bring them to the One who specializes in restoration.

Remember, Jesus will always choose compassion over compliance. When helping people conflicts with religious expectations, choose love every time.

15. How Jesus Created Buzz
~Mark 3:7-12~

Jesus departed with his disciples to the sea, and a large crowd followed from Galilee, and a large crowd followed from Judea, Jerusalem, Idumea, beyond the Jordan, and around Tyre and Sidon. The large crowd came to him because they heard about everything he was doing. Mark 3:7-8 (CSB)

BEFORE Instagram, TikTok, or YouTube, Jesus went viral the old-fashioned way—through authentic impact that people couldn't help but share. No algorithm needed, no paid promotion required. Just real transformation that spread like wildfire across ancient Palestine.

The Original Influencer

MARK paints an incredible picture: crowds streaming toward Jesus from every direction. Galilee, Judea, Jerusalem, Idumea, beyond the Jordan, around Tyre and Sidon—that's like people traveling from New York, California, Texas, Florida, and Canada just to see one person. This wasn't celebrity worship or entertainment seeking. This was desperate people who had heard that someone could actually deliver on what everyone else only promised.

The reason for the viral moment? *They heard about everything he was doing.* Not everything He was saying, posting, or promising; everything He was *doing.* Jesus' reputation wasn't built on clever content or inspirational quotes. It was built on tangible results in real people's lives.

The Crush of Authentic Influence

THE crowd became so intense that Jesus had to ask His disciples to have a boat ready *so that the crowd wouldn't crush him (Mark 3:9)*. When you're making a real difference, people will literally press in to get close to you. This wasn't polite church attendance; this was desperate hunger for genuine transformation.

Since he had healed many, all who had diseases were pressing toward him to touch him (Mark 3:10). These weren't casual followers or curious onlookers. These were people whose lives had been wrecked by sickness, demon possession, and hopelessness. They had tried everything else and found nothing that worked. But Jesus? Jesus actually delivered.

The Recognition That Matters

EVEN the demons couldn't deny Jesus' true identity. *Whenever the unclean spirits saw him, they fell down before him and cried out, "You are the Son of God!" (Mark 3:11)*. The forces of darkness recognized what many humans missed—this wasn't just another religious teacher or self-help guru. This was God in human flesh, whose presence demanded acknowledgment. But Jesus *would strongly warn them not to make him known (Mark 3:12)*. He wasn't interested in fame for fame's sake. He wasn't trying to build a personal brand or maximize His follower count. His mission was transformation, not recognition.

The Influence That Transforms

MANY times our goal is going viral, building platforms, and gaining influence. But Jesus shows us what authentic influence looks like: it's not about how many people know your name, but how many lives you've actually changed. It's not about your reach; it's about your impact.

Real influence can't be bought with marketing gimmicks or viral campaigns. It's built by serving people, caring about them, and delivering results in their lives. When you're making an impact, people see it. When you're solving problems, word of mouth happens naturally.

The Ripple Effect

JESUS' influence wasn't just wide; it was deep. People didn't just follow Him for entertainment; they followed Him for transformation. They didn't just want to be associated with Him; they wanted to be changed by Him. That's the kind of influence that lasts beyond trending topics and viral moments.

The same power that drew crowds to Jesus is available to work through you today. When you align your life with God's purposes and genuinely serve others, your influence becomes supernatural. People are drawn not to your personality but to the presence of God working through you.

CALL TO ACTION #1: Transform your influence strategy from self-promotion to genuine service. Identify three specific ways you can solve real problems for people in your sphere of influence this week. Focus on creating tangible value rather than just generating attention. Let your actions speak louder than your posts, and watch how authentic impact creates organic influence.

CALL TO ACTION #2: Leverage your current platform to point people toward Jesus rather than yourself. Use whatever influence you have—whether it's 50 followers or 50,000—to highlight God's goodness and invite others into transformation. Share stories of how God is working in your life, pray for people publicly, and create content that builds His kingdom rather than your personal brand.

16. When Jesus Slides Into Your DMs
~Mark 3:13-19~

He appointed twelve, whom he also named apostles, to be with him, to send them out to preach, and to have authority to drive out demons. Mark 3:14–15 (CSB)

HAVE you ever gotten an unexpected text from someone you admire and you're like, "Whoa, they picked me?" That surprise DM, invite, or job offer that says, "You've been seen. You've been chosen." Mark 3 gives that impression, but on a divine level.

Jesus goes up a mountain to pray, and then He calls out twelve guys by name. Not because they had it all together. Not because they were influencers or spiritual all-stars, but because He wanted to be with them and to send them out.

This is more than a "group chat" of believers; it's the original launch team for the Church. These were fishermen, tax guys, political extremists, even a future traitor. But Jesus called them anyway.

The Unlikely Squad

LOOK at this roster: Simon Peter, the impulsive fisherman who would deny Jesus three times; James and John, the "Sons of Thunder" with anger management issues; Matthew, the despised tax collector who had been ripping off his own people; Simon the Zealot, a political extremist who wanted to overthrow Rome; and Judas Iscariot, who would ultimately betray Jesus for thirty pieces of silver.

This wasn't exactly an all-star lineup. No seminary graduates. No religious credentials. No social media following. Just ordinary people with extraordinary potential in the hands of Jesus.

Jesus Still Calls Imperfect People

THIS crew wasn't impressive by religious standards, but Jesus didn't need perfect résumés. He wanted people who would walk with Him, learn from Him, and carry His message. The same is true today. God wants a willing heart, not a perfect résumé. He is in the business of making ordinary people into extraordinary vessels of His will.

He Called Them to Be with Him

BEFORE they ever preached, cast out demons, or did miracles, He called them first to simply be with Him. Notice the order in verse 14: *to be with him, to send them out to preach.* Presence with Jesus always comes before productivity for Jesus.

This is where many Christians get it backwards. We want to do great things for God without spending time with God. But relationship comes before ministry. Intimacy precedes impact. You can't give what you don't have.

Jesus Gives Power to Ordinary People

THE same authority He gave to these Twelve, to preach and drive out darkness, is available to every believer today. You may feel underqualified, but if you're walking with Jesus, you're more equipped than you think.

The Divine Selection Process

WHAT'S beautiful about Jesus' selection process is that it wasn't based on human qualifications. He didn't choose the most educated, the most talented, or the most spiritual. He chose people who were willing to follow Him, learn from Him, and be transformed by Him.

This should encourage anyone who feels like they don't have what it takes to serve God. You don't need a perfect past, a theology degree, or special talents. You just need a willing heart and a desire to be with Jesus.

The Modern Application

JESUS is still calling ordinary people to do extraordinary things. He's still looking for people who will prioritize being with Him over doing for Him. He's still giving authority to drive out darkness and preach good news to anyone willing to follow Him.

The question isn't whether you're qualified, it's whether you're available. The question isn't whether you have what it takes, it's whether you're willing to let Jesus work through you.

CALL TO ACTION #1: Seize the invitation. God has already sent your calling; it's time to RSVP with action. You don't need a title, a platform, or a Bible degree to live on mission. You just need to say yes. Start by spending time with Jesus this week, just you and Him. Then ask, "Lord, where are you sending me?" It could be your school, your workplace, or even your own home.

CALL TO ACTION #2: Delete your "too far gone" filter and start seeing people through God's perspective. Jesus chose a tax collector and a zealot to be on the same team—two people who normally would've hated each other. Who have you written off as "unlikely" or "too far gone"? Ask God to give you His eyes and open your heart to the ones He's still calling.

17. Faith Looks Foolish
~Mark 3:20-30~

When his family heard this, they set out to restrain him, because they said, "He's out of his mind." Mark 3:21 (CSB)

EVER experience that moment when friends roll their eyes at your "Jesus thing" or family members get uncomfortable with how "religious" you've become? Maybe they think you're taking this faith stuff a little too far. Welcome to the club. Jesus' own family thought He'd lost it.

In Mark 3, Jesus is so busy ministering that He can't even eat. His family shows up to pull Him out of the crowd like He's gone off the deep end. Meanwhile, religious leaders make an even darker accusation. They claim Jesus is casting out demons by the power of Satan.

When Love Looks Like Chaos

JESUS is surrounded by desperate people seeking healing, deliverance, and hope. He's working miracles, changing lives, and demonstrating the power of God. But to His family, it just looks like He's lost His mind. They're probably thinking, "This isn't the carpenter we know. This isn't normal behavior."

Sometimes following Jesus will look foolish to the people who know you best. Your old friends might not understand why you don't party like you used to. Your family might think you've become "too religious" because you actually read your Bible and pray. Your coworkers might roll their eyes when you refuse to participate in office gossip or unethical practices.

What looks like foolishness to the world often looks like faithfulness to God. When you're truly following Jesus, some people will think you've lost your mind…because in a way, you have. You've lost the mind that was focused on worldly success, temporary pleasures, and selfish ambition. You've gained the mind of Christ.

The Unforgivable Accusation

THE religious leaders took their criticism to a dangerous level. They couldn't deny Jesus' power, so they attributed it to Satan. Jesus shuts them down with simple logic: "Why would Satan fight himself?" *If a kingdom is divided against itself, that kingdom cannot stand (Mark 3:24).*

But then Jesus delivers a serious warning. Don't mess with the Holy Spirit. To say God's power is demonic is crossing a dangerous line. That level of heart-hardness is what Jesus calls the unforgivable sin. It's not about a single mistake or moment of doubt, it's about a persistent, willful rejection of God's obvious work.

The Heart Check

THE good news? If you're worried you've committed that sin, you haven't. That kind of spiritual blindness doesn't come with conviction; it comes with arrogance and apathy. If you care about your heart before God, you're in a good place.

The religious leaders' problem wasn't ignorance; it was pride. They were so invested in their own system, their own opinions, and their own understanding that they couldn't recognize God when He was standing right in front of them.

The Cost of Genuine Faith

FOLLOWING Jesus authentically will cost you some relationships and some respect. People who used to understand you might start questioning your sanity. Remember, you're in good company. If they called the Master crazy, they'll probably call His followers crazy too.

Whether people will think your faith looks foolish is a given; the real issue is whether you're willing to look foolish for the sake of following Jesus. Sometimes the most reasonable thing you can do is what others consider unreasonable.

CALL TO ACTION #1: Stand firm. This week, identify one specific area where you're hiding your faith to avoid looking "foolish"—whether it's praying before meals in public, declining an invitation that conflicts with your values, or speaking up when someone mocks Christianity.

CALL TO ACTION #2: Let God keep you tender. Pride and tradition made the religious leaders blind to the Holy Spirit. Ask God to keep your heart humble, open, and sensitive to His voice. What is the Spirit saying to you today? Are you listening?

18. Blood Doesn't Make You Family
~Mark 3:31-35~

A crowd was sitting around him and told him, "Look, your mother, your brothers, and your sisters are outside asking for you."
Mark 3:32 (CSB)

WE hear the expression "blood is thicker than water" frequently. It conveys the idea that you should always put your family first. But Jesus flips that on its head. When His mom and brothers show up outside a packed house to pull Him away, Jesus doesn't rush out. Instead, He looks around the room at His followers and says: *"Here are my mother and my brothers! Whoever does the will of God is my brother and sister and mother"* (Mark 3:34–35).

That moment wasn't a dig at His biological family; it was a defining moment for His spiritual one.

The Awkward Family Intervention

JESUS is teaching inside a crowded house, and His family is standing outside, unable to get through the crowd. They send word that they want to see Him, probably expecting Him to drop everything and come running. After all, family comes first, right?

But Jesus uses this moment to teach something revolutionary about belonging. He wasn't rejecting His relatives; He was redefining what it means to be family. In the kingdom of God, loyalty to Christ creates deeper bonds than DNA ever could.

This wasn't about disrespecting His mother Mary or dismissing His siblings. Jesus honored His earthly family throughout His life. He even made sure His mother was

45

cared for while He was dying on the cross. But He was establishing a new kind of family tree, one rooted in faith rather than genetics.

The Family You Choose

IN Jesus' day, family was everything. Your identity, your security, your future—all of it was tied to your bloodline. But Jesus was creating something unprecedented: a family based on shared faith and common purpose rather than shared DNA.

This was radical then, and it's still radical now. Jesus was saying that the bonds formed through following God together are actually stronger and more lasting than biological relationships. When you commit your life to Christ, you don't just get a Savior; you get a whole new family.

When Your Real Family Doesn't Get It

MAYBE your biological family doesn't understand your faith. Maybe they think you've gone overboard with this Jesus thing. Maybe they roll their eyes when you talk about church or get uncomfortable when you pray before meals. Jesus gets it—His own family thought He was crazy just a few verses earlier.

If you follow Jesus, you're part of a global spiritual family that spans every continent, culture, and generation. That means you belong, even if your earthly family misunderstands your faith. You have brothers and sisters in Christ who will pray for you, encourage you, and stand with you when life gets tough.

The Responsibilities of Spiritual Family

BEING part of God's family isn't just about what you receive; it's about what you give. Jesus calls us to love and support our brothers and sisters in Christ like real family because, to Him, they are real family.

This means showing up when someone needs help. It means celebrating victories and mourning losses together. It means having difficult conversations when someone is making destructive choices. It means being loyal, committed, and sacrificial in your relationships with other believers.

CALL TO ACTION #1: Don't just sit next to your spiritual family; show up for them. Who in your church community needs a word of encouragement, a meal, or a helping hand this week? Be the family Jesus says you are. Look for practical ways to demonstrate the kind of love and support that real families provide.

CALL TO ACTION #2: Lean into the spiritual family God's given you. Feeling alone in your faith? You're not. Join a small group, serve on a team, or reach out to someone for prayer today. You were never meant to walk this road solo. Take one concrete step this week to deepen your connections with your brothers and sisters in Christ.

19. You Can't Fake Fertile
~Mark 4:1-20~

And those like seed sown on good ground hear the word, welcome it, and produce fruit thirty, sixty, and a hundred times what was sown."
Mark 4:20 (CSB)

I WALKED by the home improvement store's garden center last week and was genuinely impressed. Rows of healthy green plants, immaculate flowers, not a browning leaf in the bunch. Then I noticed I was in the artificial plant section. Those plastic beauties would never need a drink, never deal with pests, and never, ever make real fruit. Sometimes the prettiest gardens are the ones that will never grow a thing.

The difference between artificial and authentic isn't always obvious at first glance—whether we're talking about plants or people. Jesus knew people were the same way with truth. That's why He told a story about a farmer tossing out seeds only to watch some get snatched up, others shrivel, and a few thrive. The seed in the story is God's Word. But the soil? That's your heart.

The Soil Test

SOME hearts are like a sidewalk, hard and unreceptive. Others are rocky, excited at first but shallow. Some are overgrown with distractions like money, anxiety, image management. And then there's the good soil—soft, deep, ready to grow something real.

Jesus wasn't just talking about first-time faith. Every time you hear God's Word, your heart is reacting in one of these four ways. So before you open your Bible or show up to church, ask, "What kind of soil am I working with today?"

That first soil type, the path where nothing penetrates, develops over time. It gets packed down by constant traffic. Your heart can develop the same hardpan layer. Every time you hear truth and don't respond, the ground gets a little more compacted.

Rocky soil is trickier to diagnose. Things actually start growing! But when the heat comes (and it always comes), the shallow root system can't sustain what looked so promising.

The Competing Crop

THEN there's the thorny ground. This soil isn't bad, it's actually quite fertile. The problem is it's growing everything. The good seed has to compete with weeds that are often more aggressive and better adapted to poor conditions.

Your heart can be like this too. Fertile enough for God's Word to take root, but so many other things are growing there that the good stuff gets choked out. Not by bad things, necessarily. Just...other things. Busy things. Urgent things that crowd out what matters most.

Good soil doesn't happen by accident. It's usually the result of things breaking down. Organic matter being worked into the ground, sometimes even the mess of last season becoming the nutrients for this one.

Spiritually, this means your failures and broken places can actually become the richest soil for God's grace to grow. The parts of your story you're most ashamed of might be exactly where His truth takes deepest root.

The Harvest Multiplication

WHEN Jesus talks about thirty, sixty, and hundredfold returns, He's describing exponential multiplication. One seed becoming hundreds of seeds.

This is what happens when God's Word finds truly fertile soil in your heart. It doesn't just change you; it produces fruit that contains seeds for changing others. Your transformation becomes the starting point for someone else's growth.

The farmer in Jesus' story doesn't get frustrated with the different soil types. He keeps sowing, knowing that some soil is ready and some isn't...yet.

God approaches your heart the same way. He's not angry about your hard places or impatient with your shallow spots. He's a Master Gardener who knows how to work with whatever soil conditions He finds.

CALL TO ACTION #1: Excavate your heart's condition. Dig deep and examine what's making it hard to receive God's Word. Uproot the rocks that need removing and yank out the weeds that need pulling. Attack this week by demanding God prepare the soil of your heart for whatever He wants to plant there.

CALL TO ACTION #2: Invest yourself as living fertilizer in someone else's spiritual garden. Just as compost enriches soil, your deliberate involvement can create breakthrough conditions for God's Word to thrive in someone's life. Choose someone around you who needs encouragement, support, or simply someone who believes in his or her potential. Pour yourself into becoming the life-giving influence that cultivates their heart into more receptive ground for God's truth.

You can't fake fertile soil, but you can cultivate it. The question isn't whether you have perfect growing conditions right now; it's whether you're willing to let the Master Gardener work on your heart until it becomes the kind of soil where His Word can take deep root and produce an abundant harvest.

20. Shine On
~Mark 4:21-25~

He also said to them, "Is a lamp brought in to be put under a basket or under a bed? Isn't it to be put on a lampstand?" Mark 4:21 (CSB)

WALKING into a dark room inevitably causes you to reach for the light switch. Nobody thinks, "You know what this room needs? More darkness." But somehow, when it comes to our faith, we act like spiritual light is optional—something we can keep hidden under our personal basket until we feel "ready" to shine.

Jesus had a different idea about how light works.

The Ridiculous Lamp

JESUS asks what seems like an obvious question: *"Is a lamp brought in to be put under a basket or under a bed?"* The answer is so clear it almost feels insulting. Of course you don't hide a lamp! That would defeat the entire purpose of having one.

But we do that with our faith. We light up in church on Sunday, then spend the rest of the week hiding our spiritual light under the basket of "keeping things private" or the bed of "not wanting to offend anyone."

Jesus is essentially saying, "You realize how ridiculous this looks, right? You're like someone who buys a flashlight and then wraps it in a blanket."

The Purpose-Built Life

LIKE infrared light, your influence is often invisible but incredibly powerful. People can't always see it, but they feel its warmth. The way you handle pressure. How you treat difficult people. The peace you carry in chaos.

People are watching to see if your faith actually works when life gets messy. Your consistent character becomes their invitation to discover what you've found.

The Use-It-or-Lose-It Principle

JESUS follows up with a warning that sounds harsh but is actually merciful: *"For whoever has, more will be given to him, and whoever does not have, even what he has will be taken away from him"* (Mark 4:25).

This isn't God being stingy; it's how spiritual muscles work. Use your faith, and it grows stronger. Hide your light, and it dims. Share what God has given you, and He gives you more to share. Keep it to yourself, and you'll discover that unused spiritual gifts have a way of atrophying.

The Compound Effect

WHEN you let your light shine, something beautiful happens: it doesn't just illuminate your immediate space, it helps others find their own light switches. Your authenticity gives others permission to be real. Your boldness inspires others to be brave. Your faith becomes contagious in the best possible way.

But when you hide your light, you're not just keeping yourself in the dark; you're leaving others to stumble around in darkness too. The light you're hiding might be exactly what someone else needs to find their way.

The Authenticity Factor

SHINING your light doesn't mean being perfect or having all the answers. It means being real about your journey—the struggles, the victories, the questions, and the discoveries.

People aren't looking for spiritual superheroes; they're looking for authentic humans who've found something worth living for.

Your story of how God has worked in your life, including the messy parts, might be the exact light someone else needs to see that God can work in their life too.

CALL TO ACTION #1: Step out of the shadows and into your spotlight moment. Identify one area where you've been hiding your faith instead of letting it shine. This week, find a specific way to let your light illuminate that space—whether it's being more open about your beliefs at work, sharing your story with a friend, or simply living with more obvious joy and authenticity.

CALL TO ACTION #2: Become a light multiplier by investing in someone else's spiritual journey. Look for someone in your life who's struggling or searching, and use your time, talents, and resources to help them discover their own light. Sometimes the best way to shine is to help others find their switch.

You weren't made to be a hidden light. You were made to light up the room, change the atmosphere, and help others find their way. It's time to get out from under that basket and start shining like you were designed to do.

21. Let God Do His Thing
~Mark 4:26-29~

"The kingdom of God is like this," he said. "A man scatters seed on the ground." Mark 4:26 (CSB)

HAVE you ever planted something and then checked it every five minutes to see if it grew? Spoiler: that's not how seeds, or souls, work.

Jesus drops a mini but mighty parable: *"The kingdom of God is like this... A man scatters seed on the ground. He sleeps and rises night and day; the seed sprouts and grows, although he doesn't know how"* (Mark 4:26-27).

You don't have to understand the process to trust it. When it comes to spiritual growth, God handles the deep work. Your role? Plant. Pray. Be present. Stay faithful.

The farmer doesn't understand the science behind growth. He just knows that if he plants good seed in good soil, growth will happen. The same is true for spiritual growth. You need to be faithful with what you can control and trust God with the rest.

Jesus describes the growth process: *"The soil produces a crop by itself: first the blade, then the head, then the full grain on the head"? (Mark 4:28)*. Notice the progression: blade, head, full grain. Each stage is necessary, and each stage takes time.

Today, we expect immediate results. We want microwave spiritual growth, but God operates on agricultural time. Real transformation happens in seasons, not seconds.

Maybe you're frustrated with your spiritual progress. You've been a Christian for years, but you still struggle with the same sins and doubts. Remember, you might be in the blade stage, but that doesn't mean God isn't working.

The farmer doesn't panic when the seed doesn't sprout overnight. He doesn't dig it up to check progress or force growth. He simply tends to what he can control and trusts the process.

This is especially important when praying for others. Maybe you've been praying for a family member's salvation for years with no visible results. The farmer's job isn't to make the seed grow. Instead, it's to create the best conditions for growth and trust God to do what only God can do. Your job is to love well and trust God's timing.

The parable ends with harvest: *"As soon as the crop is ready, he sends for the sickle, because the harvest has come" (Mark 4:29).* When God brings spiritual growth to maturity, it's unmistakable.

Don't despise the slow seasons. Trust that God is always growing something beautiful.

Growth isn't microwave quick; it's crockpot slow. Blade. Then head. Then full grain. Your job is to stay faithful while it grows.

CALL TO ACTION #1: Trust God's timeline. Release the pressure to force growth in yourself or others. Focus on faithful sowing: praying, loving, and trusting God to move.

CALL TO ACTION #2: Celebrate your progress. Don't despise the small steps. Celebrate the blade, not just the harvest.

22. God's Growth Algorithm
~Mark 4:30-34~

And he said, "With what can we compare the kingdom of God, or what parable can we use to describe it? It's like a mustard seed that, when sown upon the soil, is the smallest of all the seeds on the ground. And when sown, it comes up and grows taller than all the garden plants, and produces large branches, so that the birds of the sky can nest in its shade." Mark 4:30-32 (CSB)

EVER experience a carefully planned project getting zero recognition? Or a "brilliant" idea getting completely ignored? We are surrounded by the obsession of instant success, viral moments, and overnight sensations. But what if I told you that the most powerful movement in human history started with what looked like a complete flop?

The Original Startup Story

JESUS was essentially describing the greatest startup success story. He began with just twelve "followers" in a remote corner of the Roman Empire. Talk about humble beginnings! Today, billions of people worldwide follow Him. What looked like a failed venture on a cross became the most influential movement in human history.

The mustard seed wasn't impressive by ancient agricultural standards; it was literally the smallest seed farmers worked with. Yet it grew into something so large that birds could build entire communities in its branches. This is God's algorithm: small beginnings, exponential growth, maximum impact.

Your Small Steps Matter

AS we become more reliant on instant gratification, we often dismiss efforts that don't immediately trend. That Bible study with just three people? That one person you're mentoring? That small act of kindness that nobody noticed? God specializes in taking these "insignificant" moments and multiplying them beyond what we can imagine.

CALL TO ACTION #1: Seize the moment God is giving you to make a kingdom impact. What small step of obedience is God calling you to take this week? Start that conversation, send that text, take that risk. Remember, mustard seed faith can grow into something that provides shelter and blessing for countless others.

CALL TO ACTION #2: Upgrade from spiritual fast food to God's five-course meal—find a mentor who can help you graduate from milk to meat. In Mark 4:33-34, Jesus explained deeper truths privately to His disciples that He didn't share with the crowds. Are you growing in your understanding of God's Word through personal study and discipleship? Find someone who can help you go deeper in your faith—because the kingdom needs mature believers who can handle the "solid food" of Scripture.

23. No App For That
~Mark 4:35-41~

On that day, when evening had come, he told them, "Let's cross over to the other side." So they left the crowd and took him along since he was in the boat. And other boats were with him. A great windstorm arose, and the waves were breaking over the boat, so that the boat was already being swamped. Mark 4:35-37 (CSB)

TODAY'S therapy session got canceled. Your support system is unavailable. And the storm in your life is still raging at full intensity. We live in an age of endless self-help resources, but what happens when all our coping mechanisms fail and we're still drowning?

The Exhausted Savior

NOTICE: *He was in the stern, sleeping on the cushion (Mark 4:38a).* Jesus was so drained from ministry that He slept through a life-threatening storm. This isn't some detached deity. This is someone who understands burnout, exhaustion, and the weight of caring for people.

But when the disciples panic and wake Him with accusations, *"Teacher! Don't you care that we're going to die?" (Mark 4:38b),* Jesus doesn't respond with irritation or judgment. Instead, *He got up, rebuked the wind, and said to the sea, "Silence! Be still!" The wind ceased, and there was a great calm" (Mark 4:39).*

Authority Over Your Chaos

THE disciples' response reveals everything: *They were terrified and asked one another, "Who then is this? Even the wind and the sea obey him!" (Mark 4:41).* These weren't tourists. Several were experienced fishermen who knew dangerous weather. Yet they'd never seen anything like this.

Jesus has authority over the chaos that threatens to overwhelm you. Not just the external storms, but the internal ones too—anxiety, depression, relationship drama, financial stress, family dysfunction. The same voice that commanded wind and waves speaks peace into your situation.

CALL TO ACTION #1: Quit trying to be the captain of your own rescue mission when the Coast Guard is already on board. Jesus specializes in impossible weather. The disciples panicked and accused Jesus of not caring about their crisis, but He was literally in the boat with them the whole time. What storm are you facing right now where you need to stop managing and start trusting? Bring your current chaos to Jesus. He's not sleeping through your struggle, even when it feels like He is.

CALL TO ACTION #2: Starve your anxiety with faith instead of feeding it like a pet. What you feed grows, what you starve dies. Jesus asked, *"Why are you afraid? Do you still have no faith?" (Mark 4:40).* Fear and faith can't coexist in the same space. What specific fear is robbing you of faith right now? Name it, then remember that the One who calms storms is in your boat. Choose to trust His heart toward you, even when you can't see His hand.

Sometimes the most powerful thing Jesus does isn't removing the storm, it's staying in the boat with you through it.

24. The Villain Gets A Rewrite
~Mark 5:1-20~

As soon as he got out of the boat, a man with an unclean spirit came out of the tombs and met him. Mark 5:2 (CSB)

THERE'S always "that person"—the one everyone whispers about, the one who makes people cross the street, leave group chats, or suddenly remember they have "other plans." Maybe you've been that person—the one whose reputation precedes them, whose past defines their present, whose very presence makes others uncomfortable. What if I told you that Jesus specifically seeks out the people everyone else has written off?

Beyond Human Help

THIS man's situation was a complete disaster: *He lived in the tombs, and no one was able to restrain him anymore—not even with a chain—because he often had been bound with shackles and chains, but had torn the chains apart and smashed the shackles. No one was strong enough to subdue him. Night and day among the tombs and on the mountains, he was always crying out and cutting himself with stones* (Mark 5:3-5).

Living among the dead. Self-harming. Violent. Isolated. This wasn't someone you'd swipe right on or invite to your small group. Yet when he sees Jesus from a distance, he runs and bows before Him. Even the demons inside him recognize Jesus' authority: *"What do you have to do with me, Jesus, Son of the Most High God?"* (Mark 5:7).

The Ultimate Level-Up

AFTER Jesus casts out the demons (a whole legion of them—up to 6,000!), the townspeople find this man *sitting there, dressed and in his right mind (Mark 5:15)*. Complete transformation. Total restoration. The unparalleled before-and-after story.

But then the curveball nobody saw coming: the townspeople beg Jesus to leave! They were more concerned about their economic loss (the pigs) than this man's miraculous deliverance. Sometimes people prefer you broken because your healing challenges their comfort zones.

CALL TO ACTION #1: Believe in impossible recoveries. Expand your faith for people who seem beyond hope. Who in your life seems beyond hope—that family member, that coworker, that person from your past? The same Jesus who reached this demon-possessed man can reach anyone. Don't give up on them. Keep praying, keep believing, keep showing love. No one is beyond Jesus' reach.

CALL TO ACTION #2: Embrace your worth in Jesus' eyes instead of believing the lies about being "too far gone." Jesus specifically seeks out the people everyone else has written off, including you. Whatever shame, addiction, or brokenness you're carrying, remember that the same Jesus who reached the demon-possessed man is reaching for you today. Accept His invitation to step out of isolation and into His transforming love. You're not too damaged for His grace. Your worst chapter doesn't have to be your final story.

25. Desperate Moves, Divine Moments
~Mark 5:21-43~

One of the synagogue leaders, named Jairus, came, and when he saw Jesus, he fell at his feet and begged him earnestly, "My little daughter is dying. Come and lay your hands on her so that she can get well and live." So Jesus went with him. Mark 5:22-24 (CSB)

THE text you've been waiting for still hasn't come back. Your job application is stuck in "under review" limbo. Your prayer request feels like it's been left unread by God Himself. Our world is instant-everything, but sometimes life forces us into the most uncomfortable space of all: the waiting room. What happens when your emergency becomes someone else's interruption?

The Interruption That Changes Everything

You're a desperate father racing against time, and Jesus agrees to help. You're finally getting somewhere when suddenly—plot twist. A woman who's been bleeding for twelve years pushes through the crowd and touches Jesus' clothes. Everything stops. Jesus starts looking around asking, "Who touched me?"

Meanwhile, Jairus is probably thinking, "Are you serious right now? My daughter is DYING and you're worried about someone touching your hoodie?"

But Jesus doesn't see interruptions; He sees divine appointments. This woman had suffered for twelve years, spent all her money on doctors, and only got worse. She was ceremonially unclean, socially isolated, and completely desperate. One touch changed everything.

When Bad News Arrives

WHILE Jesus is still talking to the woman, the worst possible news arrives for Jairus: *"Your daughter is dead. Why bother the teacher anymore?" (Mark 5:35)*. Game over. Too late. But Jesus immediately responds, *"Don't be afraid. Only believe" (Mark 5:36)*.

At the house, people are already mourning. When Jesus says the girl is just sleeping, they literally laugh at Him. But Jesus takes her hand and says, *"Little girl, I say to you, get up!" (Mark 5:41)*. Instantly, she's alive, walking around, and Jesus tells them to get her some food (because even miracles make you hungry).

CALL TO ACTION #1: Find hope in God's attention to both your urgent needs and your ongoing pain. Jesus cared about the woman's twelve-year suffering just as much as Jairus' immediate emergency. God doesn't prioritize some people's pain over others. He has infinite capacity to care for every detail of your life. Bring both your crisis prayers and your chronic struggles to Him, knowing He's equally invested in your complete healing and wholeness.

CALL TO ACTION #2: Stop letting your circumstances write the obituary when Jesus is still holding the resurrection pen. "Too late" isn't in His vocabulary. Jairus heard, "Don't be afraid. Only believe," at the exact moment his worst nightmare came true. What situation in your life is requiring you to choose faith over fear right now? When circumstances scream "it's too late" or "it's impossible," remember that Jesus specializes in resurrection moments. Trust Him even when—especially when—hope seems dead.

Sometimes God's timing includes interruptions that are actually divine appointments. Your delay might be someone else's miracle.

26. When Jesus Glowed Up
~Mark 6:1-6~

"Isn't this the carpenter, the son of Mary, and the brother of James, Joses, Judas, and Simon? And aren't his sisters here with us?" So they were offended by him. Mark 6:3 (CSB)

RETURNING to your hometown after college, a new job, or a major life change exposes a flawed perception: everyone still sees you as the kid who ate glue in third grade. That was Jesus' circumstance when He returned to Nazareth.

It's like they couldn't see His transformation—that moment when someone has a major upgrade in their life, becoming more successful, confident, or accomplished than they used to be.

The Epic Rejection Story

WHEN Jesus rolled up to His hometown synagogue, the people were shaken by His wisdom and miracles. But instead of celebrating their local boy made good, they got in their feelings. "Isn't this just the carpenter? Mary's son? We know his whole family!" They couldn't get past their preconceived notions to see who Jesus had become. Their familiarity bred contempt, and they completely missed the Messiah standing right in front of them.

When Unbelief Limits the Unlimited

THIS is where it gets spicy: Jesus *was not able to do a miracle there, except that he laid his hands on a few sick people and healed them. And he was amazed at their unbelief (Mark 6:5-6).*

64

Think about that. The same Jesus who calmed storms and raised the dead was limited, not by His power, but by their lack of faith. Their unbelief created a ceiling on what God wanted to do in their community.

CALL TO ACTION #1: Revolutionize your vision of Jesus. Encounter Him as the living, powerful Savior instead of treating Him like familiar religious furniture. Maybe you've known "about" Jesus your whole life, but have you really seen Him? Ask God to give you fresh eyes to encounter Him in a new way—not as a familiar religious figure, but as the living, powerful Savior He is.

CALL TO ACTION #2: Demolish the ceiling on miracles. Let faith create space for God to move instead of doubt creating a no-fly zone. Jesus was amazed at their unbelief, and it directly impacted what He could do. What miracles, breakthroughs, or moves of God might you be missing because of your own doubt? Choose today to believe God for something bigger than your current circumstances. Your faith (or lack thereof) matters more than you think.

Don't be Nazareth. Don't let familiarity rob you of the extraordinary.

27. Sent Out With Nothing But Audacity
~Mark 6:7-13~

He summoned the Twelve and began to send them out in pairs and gave them authority over unclean spirits. Mark 6:7 (CSB)

THIS is the most important business trip of your career, but your boss tells you to leave your laptop, credit cards, and even your backup phone charger at home. "Just take your confidence and go change the world." That's basically what Jesus did when He sent out the Twelve.

The Minimalist Mission

JESUS gave His disciples authority over unclean spirits, but told them to pack like they were going on a day hike, not a ministry tour. No bread, no money, no extra clothes. Just sandals, a staff, and the power of God. This was about being completely dependent on God's provision and the hospitality of others. Working in pairs gave them companionship and credibility, but their real backup plan was divine intervention.

Notice how Jesus didn't give them a PowerPoint presentation, a stack of business cards, or even a five-year strategic plan. He gave them authority and sent them out. The disciples had no marketing budget, no social media strategy, no donor base; just the power of Christ working through ordinary people willing to be extraordinary messengers.

The Rejection Protocol

TO handle the haters, Jesus gave them a strategy: *"If any place does not welcome you or listen to you, when you leave there, shake the dust off your feet as a testimony against them" (Mark 6:11)*. This wasn't petty, it was powerful. That dust-shaking was a symbolic way of saying, "We did our part. Your response is between you and God now." No guilt trips, no manipulation, just moving on. Jesus knew rejection would come, so He prepared them upfront. This wasn't pessimism; it was realism. Not everyone would welcome the message. The disciples weren't responsible for converting hearts; they were responsible for delivering the message with boldness and love.

Mission Accomplished

THE result? Mark 6:12-13 tells us they preached repentance, cast out demons, and healed the sick. Their ministry looked exactly like Jesus' ministry because they carried His authority, not their own resources.

CALL TO ACTION #1: Step into what God is calling you to do instead of waiting until you feel "ready enough" or "equipped enough." The disciples went out with minimal provisions but maximum authority. What area of your life needs you to trust God's provision rather than relying on your own resources? Take that step.

CALL TO ACTION #2: Release the guilt you're carrying over people who have rejected your witness or walked away from faith. Like the disciples shaking off dust, remember: your job is to share the gospel, not to save people. That burden was never yours to bear.

67

28. Don't Bend, Don't Break
~Mark 6:14-29~

For Herod himself had given orders to arrest John and to chain him in prison on account of Herodias, his brother Philip's wife, because he had married her. John had been telling Herod, "It is not lawful for you to have your brother's wife." Mark 6:17-18 (CSB)

IN our age of cancel culture, getting "canceled" usually means losing your platform, your followers, or your job. But John the Baptist? He literally lost his head for calling out powerful people. Turns out, some people would rather kill the messenger than hear the message.

The Original Truth-Teller

JOHN the Baptist didn't slide into Herod's DMs with gentle suggestions. He straight-up called out the king for marrying his brother's wife—a move that was both politically dangerous and morally necessary. Herod knew John was righteous and even enjoyed listening to him, but Herodias? She held a grudge that would make your worst enemy jealous.

John wasn't trying to be controversial for the sake of controversy. He was simply doing what prophets do: speaking God's word regardless of the audience's comfort level. His boldness wasn't reckless; it was righteous. While others stayed silent to protect their positions, John prioritized obedience over self-preservation.

A Birthday Party Gone Wrong

PICTURE Herod throwing his birthday bash, feeling generous after his stepdaughter's impressive dance performance. In a moment of ego and alcohol-fueled bravado, he promises her anything she wants—up to half his kingdom.

Coached by her vengeful mother, the girl asks for John's head on a platter. Herod was "deeply distressed," but his pride wouldn't let him back down in front of his guests. One rash promise led to murder.

The Cost of Compromise

THE tragic irony: Herod knew John was righteous, yet he murdered him to save face. He chose his reputation over doing what was right. John died a martyr's death, faithful to God's truth until the very end, while Herod lived with blood on his hands.

CALL TO ACTION #1: Refuse to concede. John the Baptist died because he spoke truth to power, refusing to compromise God's standards even when it cost him everything. Are there areas where you're tempted to downplay your convictions to avoid conflict or gain approval? Stop playing it safe with your faith. Choose courage over comfort, even when the stakes feel high.

CALL TO ACTION #2: Think before you speak, and don't let pride keep you from backing down when you realize you're wrong. Herod made a rash promise that led to murder, and his pride kept him from admitting his mistake. Be careful about the commitments you make, especially when emotions are running high. Your ego isn't worth destroying lives over.

In a society that often silences truth-tellers, be like John—faithful to the end, no matter the cost.

29. Five Loaves, Zero Excuses
~Mark 6:30-44~

The apostles gathered around Jesus and reported to him all that they had done and taught. He said to them, "Come away by yourselves to a remote place and rest for a while." So they went away in the boat by themselves to a remote place." Mark 6:30-32 (CSB)

FINALLY you get a day off to chill after being exhausted from work, but then 5,000 unexpected guests show up at your house around dinnertime. Your first instinct? "There's a McDonald's down the street. Y'all figure it out." But Jesus had a different plan entirely.

The Setup

THE disciples had just returned from their ministry tour, completely drained and needing some R&R. Jesus tried to take them to a quiet spot, but the crowds followed like they were chasing a viral TikTok star. Instead of being annoyed, Jesus had compassion on them because they were like sheep without a shepherd.

When evening came and stomachs started growling, the disciples suggested the obvious solution: send everyone away to buy food. But Jesus dropped a bombshell: *"You give them something to eat"* (Mark 6:37).

The Math Wasn't Mathing

FEEDING the crowd would cost 200 denarii, about eight months' salary, according to the Twelve. They were basically saying, "Jesus, we'd need to take out a second mortgage to feed these people!"

But Jesus wasn't asking about their bank account. He asked what they already had: five loaves and two fish. A kid's lunch. Literally the most inadequate meal for the most impossible situation.

The Miracle in the Method

JESUS didn't create food from thin air. He took what was already there, that small lunch, blessed it and multiplied it beyond imagination. Everyone ate until they were satisfied, and there were twelve baskets of leftovers. One basket for each disciple, as if God was saying, "See? I had this covered all along."

CALL TO ACTION #1: Offer God what you have instead of telling Him what you can't do. The disciples focused on what they lacked (money), but God wanted to use what they possessed (a boy's lunch). What small resource, talent, or opportunity are you dismissing as "not enough"? Bring it to Jesus and watch Him multiply it beyond your wildest expectations.

CALL TO ACTION #2: Take responsibility when others want to walk away. When faced with 5,000 hungry people, the disciples' first instinct was to send them somewhere else: "This isn't our problem." But Jesus challenged them: *"You give them something to eat."* What overwhelming need is right in front of you that everyone else is avoiding? Instead of looking for an exit strategy, ask God how He wants to use you in the solution. Sometimes the miracle begins, not with what's in your hands, but with your willingness to stay and engage when everyone else wants to leave.

30. You're Being Grown
~Mark 6:45-52~

Immediately he made his disciples get into the boat and go ahead of him to the other side, to Bethsaida, while he dismissed the crowd. Mark 6:45 (CSB)

HAVE you ever felt like God disappeared right when you needed Him most? Like you're fighting battles alone while He's somewhere else, apparently too busy to notice your struggle?

The disciples knew that feeling. They just witnessed Jesus feed five thousand people with a kid's lunch—the kind of miracle that should have them feeling invincible. But instead of celebrating, Jesus immediately sends them away. "Get in the boat," He tells them. "Go to the other side. I'll catch up later." So they obey, probably expecting a peaceful evening cruise across familiar waters. But the Sea of Galilee had other plans.

The Storm That Came from Nowhere

BY evening, they're fighting for their lives. The wind is against them, waves are crashing over the boat, and they're making zero progress despite hours of rowing. Their arms are burning, their backs are aching, and they're starting to wonder if they're going to make it to shore at all.

Meanwhile, where's Jesus? On a mountain, praying. Alone. While they're down in the valley, battling the storm of their lives.

It's the kind of situation that makes you question everything. If Jesus really cares, why isn't He here? If He has the power to calm storms, why is He letting this one rage?

But what they couldn't see from their position in the boat: Jesus was watching them the entire time. Mark 6:48 tells us He *saw them straining at the oars.* He wasn't absent; He was observing. He wasn't ignoring their struggle; He was allowing it for a purpose.

Around three in the morning (the darkest, most exhausting part of their ordeal), Jesus finally makes His move. But He doesn't rush to rescue them. He walks. On the water. Like it's solid ground.

The Voice That Changes Everything

THE disciples' first reaction? Terror. They think He's a ghost. After hours of feeling abandoned, when Jesus finally shows up, they don't recognize Him. Sometimes when we're in survival mode, we can't see God even when He's right in front of us.

But then Jesus speaks: *"Have courage! It is I. Don't be afraid"* (Mark 6:50). Those three words, *"It is I,"* are the same phrase God used when Moses asked His name at the burning bush. This wasn't just Jesus identifying Himself; it was a declaration of His divine nature.

The Growth That Comes Through Struggle

WHY did Jesus let them struggle for so long? Because sometimes the storm isn't the problem; it's the classroom.

The disciples needed to learn that Jesus' presence doesn't always prevent difficulties, but it does provide peace in the midst of them. If Jesus had prevented the storm, the disciples would have missed one of the most important lessons of their lives.

The struggle wasn't punishment; it was preparation. Every stroke of the oars was building their endurance. Every hour of uncertainty was developing their faith. Every moment of feeling alone was teaching them to recognize God's presence in new ways.

The beautiful truth is that Jesus never actually left them. Even when He was on the mountain praying, He was interceding for them. Even when they couldn't see Him, He was watching over them. Even when they felt abandoned, they were never alone.

Sometimes God's presence feels distant, not because He's moved away, but because He's working in ways we don't expect. He's not ghosting us; He's growing us.

The Peace That Defies Logic

WHEN Jesus stepped into the boat, the wind immediately ceased. Not gradually. Immediately. The storm that had been raging for hours was calmed in an instant.

But notice the order. First Jesus got in the boat, then the storm ceased. His presence preceded the peace. Sometimes we want the peace without the presence, the calm without the relationship. But Jesus doesn't just fix our circumstances—He transforms our perspective.

CALL TO ACTION #1: Trust the process even when you can't see the purpose. God often uses storms to develop our faith muscles and deepen our dependence on Him. What current struggle might actually be a classroom where God is teaching you something essential? Instead of just praying for the storm to end, ask what He wants you to learn while you're in it.

CALL TO ACTION #2: Let Jesus into your boat instead of just asking Him to calm your storm. He's not just a problem-solver; He's the Prince of Peace who wants to be present in your struggle. Invite Him into your situation rather than trying to row through life's storms alone.

You're not ghosted; you're being grown. The same Jesus who walked on water is walking into your storm, and when He steps into your boat, everything changes.

31. Rippling Faith
~Mark 6:53-56

Wherever he went, into villages, towns, or the country, they laid the sick in the marketplaces and begged him that they might touch just the end of his robe. And everyone who touched it was healed.
Mark 6:56 (CSB)

FAITH is contagious. In this brief but powerful passage, we see crowds so convinced of Jesus' power that they don't ask for His time or words. Just a brush of His cloak. Word must have spread from the woman with the issue of blood; someone heard her story, believed it, and passed it on. Now, the streets are filled with people acting on secondhand faith. That kind of chain reaction still happens today.

The stage is set: entire marketplaces transformed into outdoor hospitals. People carrying their sick relatives on stretchers, mats, and makeshift beds. The desperation was palpable, but so was the hope. These weren't casual seekers or curious onlookers. These were people who had run out of other options and were betting everything on one encounter with Jesus.

Our society is flooded with information, but starving for encounters. The people who gathered around Jesus weren't showing up to hear another opinion. They were showing up for transformation. And they were bold enough to believe that the same power that worked for one woman could still work for them.

One touch. One act of belief. One story about healing. And it multiplies.

What's remarkable is that Jesus didn't seem overwhelmed by the constant reaching, grabbing, and pressing in. He welcomed it. He made Himself available to every desperate hand that stretched toward Him. There was no VIP section, no appointment necessary, no screening process. Just open access to divine power for anyone willing to reach out in faith.

You may not feel like your faith is impressive. Maybe it feels tired, quiet, or inconsistent. But when you put it in motion, even by just reaching for Jesus in your pain, it sends a signal to others. You don't have to preach to start a ripple. You just have to be seen reaching.

Faith doesn't need a spotlight. It just needs motion. When others see you reaching for Jesus in your anxiety, your grief, your confusion, they begin to believe they can too. And that's when healing spreads. Not through charisma, but through quiet desperation that still reaches. And Jesus responds to it every time.

Consider how many people in your circle are watching to see if faith actually works. They're observing how you handle pressure, disappointment, and uncertainty. Your willingness to reach toward Jesus in those raw places gives them permission to do the same. Your vulnerability becomes their invitation.

The woman with the issue of blood never intended to start a movement. She just wanted to get well. But her story became the catalyst for countless others to believe that healing was possible. Your story of reaching for Jesus could do the same.

CALL TO ACTION #1: Reach out in your own need today. What area of your life feels sick, stuck or ignored? Don't talk yourself out of it; pray boldly and reach out in faith, even if it's small.

CALL TO ACTION #2: Invite someone to experience what changed you. Whether it's a church service, a small group, or a conversation over coffee, give someone access to the space where your healing started.

32. The Recipe Doesn't Matter
~Mark 7:1-23~

This people honors me with their lips, but their heart is far from me.
Mark 7:6 (CSB)

WE all know that friend who's obsessed with fancy restaurants. They can tell anyone about every ingredient, the chef's background, how the dish was prepared. But when they cook at home, it's terrible. Knowledge without skill.

That's basically what Jesus walked into with the religious leaders. They had the spiritual presentation down to an art form, but something was off.

When Perfect Gets Hollow

THE Pharisees came at Jesus because His disciples ate without the ceremonial handwashing. Not basic hygiene. This was about religious theater, the kind of performance that makes people look holy while their hearts stay cold.

These guys had turned simple meals into elaborate rituals. Every gesture had meaning, every step required precision. They'd created a whole system of spiritual choreography that looked impressive but missed the point.

Jesus wasn't having it. He called them out for caring more about looking spiritual than connecting with God. They had turned faith into a performance review instead of a relationship. Anyone can follow every spiritual routine, hit every religious checkpoint, and still be empty inside. Going through the motions while the heart checks out.

The Contamination Problem

HERE'S where Jesus flipped their understanding. They obsessed over external cleanliness while ignoring the mess inside their hearts. Jesus listed what corrupts us: *evil thoughts, sexual immorality, theft, murder, adultery, greed, evil actions, deceit, self-indulgence, envy, slander, pride, and foolishness (Mark 7:21-22).* That's the real contamination. Not unwashed hands, but unwashed hearts. We still do this. Worry about how we look in church while harboring bitterness. Stress about saying the right words while treating people poorly. Focus on spiritual appearances while our character stays broken. It's like scrubbing the outside of a cup while leaving the inside filthy. The Pharisees had mastered external religion but ignored internal transformation.

What Actually Matters

GOD wants authenticity, not performance. He's not impressed by spiritual résumés if life doesn't match. He'd rather have an honest mess than fake perfection. When faith has substance, people notice. Not because someone is performing spirituality, but because something is really happening in their life. People can tell the difference. That's what draws people to Jesus. Faith changes how someone treats their family, handles stress, responds to criticism. It shows up in moments when nobody's watching.

CALL TO ACTION #1: Get honest about what's fake. Stop performing spirituality and start living it. Where is the concern with looking good overpowering being good? Pick an area this week and choose authenticity over appearance.

CALL TO ACTION #2: Let life speak louder than words. Instead of trying to impress people with how spiritual your words sound, love them. Character matters more than vocabulary.

33. I'll Take The Crumbs
~Mark 7:24-30~

But she replied to him, "Lord, even the dogs under the table eat the children's crumbs." Mark 7:28 (CSB)

FEEL like God's blessings are for other people? The polished ones. The ones with the church background, the perfect story, the spiritual résumé? Like you're standing outside the restaurant watching everyone else enjoy the feast while you're left with whatever scraps might fall through the cracks?

This Gentile woman knew that feeling intimately. She was everything the religious establishment would consider unqualified—wrong ethnicity, wrong gender, wrong social status. But her daughter was tormented by a demon, and she'd heard about this Jewish teacher who had power over evil spirits. So she did what desperate mothers do: she went after help, regardless of the obstacles.

When she found Jesus, He was trying to get some rest in a house where He thought He could remain hidden. But she tracked Him down anyway. This woman didn't wait for an invitation or worry about proper protocol. She barged into His temporary retreat and fell at His feet, begging Him to cast the demon out of her daughter.

Her approach was bold, desperate, and completely inappropriate by cultural standards. But she didn't care about social conventions; she cared about her daughter's freedom.

This is what real faith looks like when it's stripped of religious pretense. It's raw, urgent, and willing to break social rules for the sake of breakthrough.

RYAN HELLER

The Test That Revealed Heart

JESUS' response seems harsh at first: *"Let the children be fed first, because it isn't right to take the children's bread and throw it to the dogs"* (Mark 7:27). He was using a common Jewish metaphor where *children* referred to the Jewish people and *dogs* referred to Gentiles. But this wasn't cruelty; it was a test. Jesus was giving her an opportunity to demonstrate the kind of faith that moves His heart.

Her response revealed everything about her character: *"Lord, even the dogs under the table eat the children's crumbs."* She didn't argue with the metaphor or get defensive about being called a dog. Instead, she embraced it and turned it into an argument for why she deserved help.

What this woman understood is revolutionary: even the smallest portion of Jesus' power is enough to transform everything. She wasn't asking for the full meal, just the crumbs that fell from the table.

This is crumb theology at its finest. When you recognize that even the leftovers from Jesus' table are more powerful than anything else the world has to offer, you become grateful for whatever He's willing to give rather than demanding the full portion.

The Faith That Moves Mountains

HER response amazed Jesus. *"Because of this reply, you may go. The demon has left your daughter"* (Mark 7:29). He didn't need to travel to her house, lay hands on the girl, or perform any visible miracle. Her faith was so compelling that He healed her daughter from a distance with just a word.

This woman's faith was humble, persistent, creative, and desperate. She was willing to be embarrassed, rejected, or misunderstood if it meant getting help for her daughter.

When the woman returned home, she found her daughter lying peacefully on the bed, completely free from the demon that had tormented her. The healing was instant

80

and complete—just total transformation through the power of crumb-sized faith.

The Access That Grace Provides

WHAT this story teaches us is that God's kingdom operates on an overflow principle. There's so much abundance at His table that even the crumbs are enough to satisfy our deepest needs. We don't have to compete for His attention or earn our way to the main course.

This should encourage anyone who feels like they're on the outside looking in. Maybe you don't have the right background, the perfect testimony, or the impressive spiritual résumé. But this woman's story proves that crumbs from Jesus are better than banquets from anywhere else.

The truth is that through Jesus, we're no longer dogs begging for crumbs; we're children invited to the table. But this woman's story reminds us that even when we feel like outsiders, God's grace is sufficient.

CALL TO ACTION #1: Approach Jesus boldly instead of letting your background or brokenness keep you away. Your access to Him isn't based on your worthiness. It's based on His grace. This woman had every reason to feel disqualified, but she came anyway. What's keeping you from bringing your desperate needs to Jesus? Start asking with the confidence that His crumbs are enough to change everything.

CALL TO ACTION #2: Embrace crumb-sized faith and watch God work miracles. Don't let apparent rejection or delayed answers discourage you from continuing to seek Him. How can you respond to God's apparent silence or difficult circumstances with the same kind of creative, persistent trust? Keep asking, keep seeking, keep knocking. Even the crumbs from His table are worth the wait.

34. From Silent Mode to Spirit-Lit
~Mark 7:31-37~

Looking up to heaven, he sighed deeply and said to him, "Ephphatha!" (that is, "Be opened!"). Mark 7:34 (CSB)

LIFE can put you on silent mode—no spiritual signal, no emotional volume. You show up to church, open your Bible, even pray…but it all feels muted. You're not hearing God, and you're not sure what to say back. The words are there, but they're not connecting.

That's exactly where this man was. Deaf. Mute. Stuck in silence. Surrounded by sound and conversation but unable to participate in either. He could see people's lips moving, watch their animated discussions, observe their laughter and tears, but he was locked out of the audio experience of life.

The Friends Who Wouldn't Give Up

WHAT'S beautiful about this story is that the man didn't come to Jesus alone. Mark tells us *they brought* him and they *begged Jesus* to help him. When you're stuck in silence, you need friends who will speak for you, advocate for you, and refuse to let you stay isolated.

These friends had heard about Jesus' power to heal, and they weren't going to let their friend's disability keep him from experiencing that power. They became his voice when he had none, his faith when his might had been weak, his hope when despair seemed reasonable.

The Personal Touch

JESUS could have healed this man with a word from a distance, like He did with the Gentile woman's daughter. But instead, He chose to make it personal. He took the man aside, away from the crowd, and engaged with him in the most intimate way possible.

Jesus put His fingers in the man's ears and touched his tongue. For someone who had been isolated by his disabilities, this physical contact must have been profound. Jesus wasn't afraid to get close, to touch what was broken, to enter into the man's world of silence.

The Sigh That Revealed God's Heart

THEN Jesus did something remarkable: He locked up to heaven and sighed deeply. This wasn't a sigh of frustration or impatience. It was a sigh of compassion, of grief over the brokenness of the world, of empathy for human suffering.

That sigh revealed the heart of God toward our pain. He's not distant or detached from our struggles. He's moved by our brokenness, grieved by our isolation, and motivated by love to do something about it.

Then Jesus spoke one word: *"Ephphatha!"* which means *"Be opened!"* It wasn't a long prayer or a complicated ritual. It was a simple command spoken with divine authority. And immediately, the man's ears were opened and his tongue was released.

The Immediate Transformation

THE healing was instant and complete. The man who had never heard clearly could suddenly distinguish every sound. The tongue that had been tied was suddenly free to form words perfectly. There was no gradual improvement or partial healing—just immediate, total transformation.

This is what happens when Jesus unmutes your life. The spiritual ears that couldn't hear His voice suddenly pick up every whisper. The heart that couldn't express worship suddenly overflows with praise. The life that felt stuck in silence suddenly becomes a symphony of God's grace.

CALL TO ACTION #1: Boldly ask God to break through your spiritual silence and restore full communication. The same Jesus who opened deaf ears and released mute tongues is ready to unmute your life. What areas of your spiritual life feel stuck in silent mode? Where do you need God to speak, *"Ephphatha,"* over your circumstances? This week, boldly ask Him to open your ears to hear His voice clearly and release your voice to declare His goodness.

CALL TO ACTION #2: Become the friend who carries others into Jesus' presence when they can't get there alone. Just as this man's friends brought him to Jesus and advocated for his healing, identify someone in your life who needs you to be their voice, their faith, their hope. Carry them in prayer, bring them into community, and refuse to let them stay isolated in their struggles.

35. Power Moves
~Mark 8:1-10~

"I have compassion on the crowd, because they've already stayed with me three days and have nothing to eat." Mark 8:2 (CSB)

SCROLLING through social media reveals a GoFundMe for someone's medical bills that's been up for weeks with only $47 raised. Your heart sinks. That gut-punch feeling? That's how Jesus felt when He saw 4,000 hungry people who'd been camping out for three days just to be near Him. But while we might hit "share" and keep scrolling, Jesus did something that literally fed the multitude.

Families with children, elderly people, individuals who had walked miles just to hear Jesus teach. They hadn't planned to stay this long, but His words were so compelling they couldn't leave. Now they were far from home, exhausted, and running on empty.

When Compassion Becomes Action

IN Mark 8:1-10, we witness Jesus' second miraculous feeding. This time, He's in Gentile territory, showing that God's love doesn't have geographic boundaries or cultural limitations. The crowd had been with Him for three days, and Jesus felt their hunger in His bones.

The Greek word for *compassion* here literally means "to be moved in your intestines." It's that deep, visceral response when you see someone hurting. Jesus didn't just feel bad for them; He was physically moved by their need. Revolutionary: He didn't wait for them to ask. He saw the need and acted.

85

Notice how Jesus operates. He takes what seems impossibly small (seven loaves and a few fish for 4,000 people), gives thanks for it, and multiplies it beyond imagination. Seven basketfuls of leftovers? That's not just provision; that's Abundance (with a capital A)!

The Culture Shift We Need

OUR digital-age, instant-gratification lifestyle has turned us into experts at numbing ourselves to others' pain. We see homelessness and look away. We hear about global hunger and change the channel. We know our neighbors are struggling, but we're "too busy" to check in.

But Jesus shows us a different way. Real compassion isn't just feeling; it's seeing a need and asking, "What do I have that God can use?" Maybe it's not seven loaves, but it could be your time, your skills, your platform, or your resources.

The disciples' response is so relatable: "How can anyone feed these people in this remote place?" In other words, "This is impossible, Jesus." But Jesus doesn't ask us to figure out the how; He asks us to bring the what. What do you have? Bring it. Give thanks for it. Watch Him multiply it.

CALL TO ACTION #1: Act on your compassion. For the next 24 hours, ask God to break your heart for what breaks His. When you feel that gut-level compassion for someone, don't just feel it. Act on it. Text that person. Make that donation. Start small, but start.

CALL TO ACTION #2: Inventory your "loaves and fishes." List what you have that God could multiply. Your network? Your creativity? Your skills? Stop focusing on what you lack and start thanking God for what you have. Then ask Him how He wants to use it.

36. Tiny Thoughts Corrupt Big Faith
~Mark 8:11-21~

"Watch out! Beware of the leaven of the Pharisees and the leaven of Herod." Mark 8:15 (CSB)

IT takes just a few mold spores to contaminate an entire loaf of bread. You buy a fresh loaf and store it away, but a couple days later you notice a tiny green spot. You might consider cutting around it, but by the next day the contamination has spread throughout the entire loaf. What started as a small infection corrupted the whole thing. The same principle applies to toxic mindsets. Herod and the Pharisees represented two infectious faith conversations.

Jesus issues a yeast warning, code word for malignant influence. *"Watch out! Beware of the yeast of the Pharisees and the yeast of Herod."* The Pharisees were infected with performance-based faith culture. They attempted to demonstrate spiritual superiority by inventing extra rules to obey. Herod represented political influence and self-preservation by any means. Two distinct infections corrupting the faith conversation. The disciples assumed He meant bread since they had forgotten lunch.

Jesus intensifies the questioning: *"Why are you discussing the fact you have no bread? Don't you understand or comprehend? Do you have hardened hearts? Do you have eyes and not see; do you have ears and not hear? And do you not remember?" (Mark 8:17-18).*

He calls them to remember miracles: 5,000 fed with 5 loaves; 12 baskets collected. 4,000 fed with 7 loaves; 7 baskets collected. They had witnessed God's power twice and still worried about lunch. Their belief system had been infected with scarcity and doubt.

The yeast of the Pharisees was religious pride in the guise of spiritual maturity. They demanded a sign while ignoring glaring signs of God at work around them. Their worldview was so infected they missed the Messiah.

Herod's yeast was political pragmatism over spiritual conviction. He beheaded John to save face, favoring reputation over righteousness. This mindset values image over integrity, popularity over principle, and temporary over eternal.

Both infections are silent and gradual. You don't wake up sick. It creeps in through little compromises and seemingly innocuous attitudes. Poisoned worldviews feel normal to us.

Jesus didn't solve this by bombarding them with information but by helping them remember. The antidote for corrupted worldviews is recollection of God's faithfulness. When fear whispers, "God will not provide," remember the miracles. When pride whispers, "You're more spiritual than that person," recall you're saved by grace. When compromise whispers, "Just be practical," remember God is above us and His ways are higher than ours.

CALL TO ACTION #1: Check your heart for dangerous trends trying to colonize your faith cloaked as common sense but cultivating toxicity. What mindsets are you tolerating that sound logical? Fear masked as prudence? Pride masquerading as wisdom? Name it and nip it.

CALL TO ACTION #2: Commit to cultivating your belief system intentionally rather than letting it become infected by cultural poisons. Dilute toxic influences with Scripture, worship, community, and testimony of God's faithfulness. Protect your faith.

37. The Second Touch
~Mark 8:22-26~

Again Jesus placed his hands on the man's eyes… and he saw everything clearly. Mark 8:25 (CSB)

YOUR breakthrough is buffering. You've started healing, but you're still not whole. It's as though you're downloading something important when your internet starts acting up. The progress bar moves forward, then stalls. You're getting somewhere, but not fast enough. You can see partial results, but you're still waiting for the complete image to load. That is demonstrated in this remarkable healing story, the only two-stage miracle in all the Gospels.

The Unusual Approach

SOME people brought a blind man to Jesus in Bethsaida, begging Him to touch their friend. But instead of healing him instantly in front of the crowd, Jesus did something unexpected: He took the man by the hand and led him outside the village, away from the spectators. This wasn't about creating a public spectacle or building His platform. This was about personal, intimate restoration that required privacy and process.

Jesus spit on the man's eyes and placed His hands on him—a deeply personal, physical interaction. Then He asked, *"Do you see anything?"* (Mark 8:23). The man's response reveals the partial nature of his healing: *"I see people—they look like trees walking around"* (Mark 8:24).

The Blurry In-Between

THIS is the awkward middle stage that most of us can relate to. The man could see, but not clearly. He had vision, but not focus. He could distinguish movement and shapes, but couldn't make out details or faces. He was no longer completely blind, but he wasn't fully sighted either.

How many of us are living in this blurry in-between space? You've experienced God's touch in your life—you know He's real, you've seen Him work—but you're still waiting for complete clarity. You can see God moving, but the details are fuzzy. You know healing has begun, but you're not fully whole yet. Maybe you've been delivered from addiction, but you still struggle with temptation. Perhaps God has restored your marriage, but you're still working through trust issues. You might have found your calling, but you're still developing the skills to walk in it fully.

The Second Touch

THE beauty of this story is that Jesus didn't walk away after the partial healing. *Again Jesus placed his hands on the man's eyes. The man looked intently and his sight was restored and he saw everything clearly (Mark 8:25)*. Jesus wasn't frustrated with the man's incomplete vision. He wasn't disappointed that the first touch didn't produce perfect results. He simply provided what was needed for complete restoration. This is the only recorded two-stage healing in the Gospels, and it wasn't because Jesus lacked power. Every other healing was instantaneous and complete. This gradual restoration was intentional—a living parable about how spiritual growth often works.

The Process of Transformation

SOMETIMES God heals instantly, completely. Other times, He works progressively, allowing us to adjust to new levels

90

of spiritual sight gradually. Both approaches reflect His wisdom and love. Our spiritual transformation often follows the same pattern. God doesn't change everything about us overnight because we couldn't handle the complete transformation all at once. He works progressively, helping us grow into the fullness of what He's called us to become.

The Patience of the Healer

WHAT is most striking about this story is Jesus' patience with the process. He didn't seem surprised or disappointed that the first touch produced partial results. He simply continued the work until it was complete. This reveals something beautiful about God's character: He's not frustrated with your incomplete transformation. He's not disappointed that you're still growing. He's not impatient with your blurry vision. God is committed to finishing what He started in your life. The same hands that began your healing will complete it. The same power that gave you spiritual sight will continue to bring clarity and focus.

CALL TO ACTION #1: Pursue the second touch instead of settling for partial breakthroughs. Don't settle for blurry spiritual vision when God wants to give you complete clarity. Identify areas where you've experienced partial growth but still need God's continued work. Keep coming back to Jesus for the next level of transformation instead of accepting "good enough" as the final result.

CALL TO ACTION #2: Practice patience with your spiritual development and others' growth. Celebrate progress you see, even when it's unclear. Trust God is working in your life and isn't finished. Give others grace you need for blurry seasons. Sometimes the most powerful thing Jesus does isn't removing but staying present. The hands that gave partial sight will complete the work. Keep coming for the second touch.

38. The Trick Question
~Mark 8:27-30~

"But you," he asked them, *"who do you say that I am?"*
Mark 8:29 (CSB)

STUDYING all night, reviewing notes, highlighting important parts, even making flashcards allows you to walk into class feeling confident until the teacher hands out the test and you see that one question that makes your stomach drop. It looks simple, but something about it feels like a trap. Like your answer will reveal way more than you intended. It was the same when Jesus asked His disciples the question that changed everything.

Like any good teacher, Jesus started with the easy stuff. He asked first, *"Who do people say that I am?"* (Mark 8:27). The disciples could handle that one. It was just reporting what they'd heard. John the Baptist. Elijah. One of the prophets. Safe answers.

These were the kind of answers you give when you're sitting in the back row, hoping not to get called on. Academic. Distant. But then Jesus made it personal.

Peter blurts out the answer: *"You are the Messiah"* (Mark 8:29). In that moment, Peter wasn't just giving the right answer; he was betting his entire future on it. Calling someone the Messiah was declaring them to be God's chosen deliverer, the one Israel had been waiting for.

Jesus' question reveals your entire personality based on how you respond. Your answer doesn't just show what you think about Jesus; it exposes your worldview, your priorities, your understanding of reality.

If Jesus is just a good teacher, His words are suggestions you can take or leave. If He's a prophet, His message is important but not necessarily binding. But if He's the Messiah, if He's God in human flesh, everything changes. Your money, relationships, career, entire life becomes subject to His authority.

What's terrifying and beautiful about following Jesus is that life becomes an open book test where your answers are revealed through your choices. You can say Jesus is Lord on Sunday, but Monday through Saturday shows whether you really believe it.

Two thousand years later, Jesus is still asking the same question. Every generation has to answer. You can't stay neutral on Jesus.

Jesus isn't looking for perfect theological precision. He's looking for honest recognition. Peter's answer wasn't sophisticated; it was simple and true. *"You are the Messiah."*

CALL TO ACTION #1: Answer with your life, not just your lips. Jesus isn't asking for the answer you think He wants to hear. He's asking for what you actually believe. Take time this week to honestly examine your response. What do you believe about who Jesus is?

CALL TO ACTION #2: Transform your confession into your lifestyle. The same Jesus you call Messiah on Sunday should influence your Monday decisions. This week, identify one area where your actions don't match your beliefs about Jesus. Make the necessary changes to live consistently.

39. Is God's Plan Defeat?
~Mark 8:31-33~

"You are not thinking about God's concerns but human concerns."
Mark 8:33b (CSB)

CONSIDER a time when you expected events to go one way, and they went the exact opposite. Maybe you lined up everything perfectly; set the goal, made the plan, followed the steps, but the outcome still felt like a loss. It is easy to carry that same mindset into our faith, believing God will always work in straight lines and clean victories.

Peter had expectations too. He had seen Jesus do amazing activities: feed thousands, walk on water, command storms. So when Jesus started talking about rejection, suffering, and death, Peter was quick to step in and correct Him. This couldn't possibly be part of the plan. Kings conquer; they don't die.

But Jesus wasn't confused. He knew what He was walking into. And instead of entertaining Peter's human reaction, He called it out. Not because Peter was evil, but because his mindset had shifted from trust to personal preference.

Peter's response reveals something deeply human about how we process disappointment. When our expectations don't align with God's revealed plan, we often assume God needs correction rather than considering that our perspective might be limited. Peter couldn't fathom a Messiah who would suffer because suffering felt like failure to him.

That's where we find ourselves. We want God's power, but not His process. We love His promises, but we challenge His path when it doesn't look like success. When we reward immediate results, we can forget that faith often flourishes through waiting, disappointment, even defeat.

The cross was never a failure. It wasn't a mistake or a detour. It was divine strategy. That same wisdom operates in your life today. God's plan may confuse your senses, but it will never betray His purposes. What looks like loss often becomes the foundation for God's greatest victories.

Consider how God's greatest works looked like defeats before they became triumphs. Joseph's imprisonment preceded his promotion. David's exile prepared him for kingship. Israel's captivity led to restoration. The pattern repeats: apparent loss followed by unexpected gain.

So when life feels upside-down, when the dream dies, when the job falls through, when the healing doesn't come, that doesn't mean God is absent. It might mean He is closer than ever, working through pain to bring resurrection life. His timeline rarely matches ours, but His faithfulness never wavers.

The difference between human concerns and God's concerns often comes down to perspective and timing. We see immediate circumstances; He sees the eternal outcome. We focus on comfort; He prioritizes character. We want relief; He wants relationship. Learning to trust His concerns requires surrendering our need to understand everything and embracing faith in His goodness.

CALL TO ACTION #1: Shift your perspective. Take time today to ask God where your expectations have been shaped more by emotions or cultural values than by His Word. Ask Him to help you see through His eyes.

CALL TO ACTION #2: Trust the long game. Jesus never promised quick fixes. He promised His presence. Keep showing up. Keep walking, even when the road looks like loss. The cross was Friday, but Sunday changed everything.

40. Why Following Jesus Isn't Safe
~Mark 8:34-38~

"If anyone wants to follow after me, let him deny himself, take up his cross, and follow me." Mark 8:34 (CSB)

THERE are two types of Christians, and only one of them is actually dangerous.

Cultural Christians have Christian traditions, values, and practices that are based on family, community, or personal preferences rather than an intimate experience with Jesus Christ. You went to a Christian school or your grandmother dragged you to church. It's external influence creating internal compliance. Safe. Predictable.

Convictional Christians have a Christian worldview because they are convicted by God and the Bible. They are prompted and led by the Holy Spirit. It's personal and significant. They don't live a certain way to please others; they do so because God put it into their heart. These change the world.

Jesus spoke these words in Mark 8:34 immediately after Peter's confession and Jesus' first prediction of His death. The disciples were expecting a conquering king, but Jesus was describing a suffering servant.

The phrase *take up his cross* would have been shocking to the disciples. The cross was a Roman instrument of execution for the worst criminals. It meant public humiliation, excruciating pain, and certain death. When Jesus said, *"Take up your cross,"* He wasn't speaking metaphorically about minor inconveniences. He was talking about willingness to die for the gospel.

This is where the line gets drawn between cultural and convictional Christianity. Taking up your cross is being a convictional Christian. Convictional Christians are willing to sweat and suffer for the kingdom of God. It's in them. Cultural Christians want the benefits without the cost.

Following Jesus isn't safe because it demands everything. Not "do what makes you happy" but "die to what makes you selfish." Self-denial isn't just a digital detox. It's a daily decision to abandon your agenda and follow His.

The cross isn't just the price we pay to get the good stuff. The cross is the good stuff. The life Jesus offers is infinitely better than anything you're giving up. But you can't experience that life while death-gripping the old one.

Here's the uncomfortable truth: cultural Christians aren't really Christians at all. Jesus didn't say, "If anyone wants to follow after me, let him keep his family traditions and church attendance." He said, *"Take up his cross and follow me."* Without the cross, there's no Christianity. Without sacrifice, there's no salvation.

CALL TO ACTION #1: Answer your spiritual alarm clock. Identify one area where you've been cultural instead of convictional. Make the hard decision to turn away from comfortable Christianity and embrace the cross.

CALL TO ACTION #2: Get brutally honest with yourself. Are you following Jesus for the aesthetic or for real? The world doesn't need more comfortable Christians; it needs convictional Christians willing to die to themselves so Christ can live through them.

41. When Elon Is Your Uber Driver
~Mark 9:1-13~

"There are some standing here who will not taste death until they see the kingdom of God come in power." Mark 9:1 (CSB)

IMAGINE ordering an Uber and some regular-looking guy picks you up in a beat-up Honda Civic. You're making small talk when he casually mentions he's launching rockets to Mars next week. You laugh, thinking he's joking, until he shows you his phone and you realize you've been riding with Elon Musk. That moment when you discover someone's true identity changes everything. That was the experience of Peter, James, and John on a mountainside.

The Greatest Identity Reveal

JESUS had been their teacher, friend, and traveling companion for months. They'd seen Him tired, hungry, even frustrated. He looked like any other Jewish carpenter from a small town. But then, on this mountain, everything changed.

Mark 9:2 tells us Jesus was transfigured before them. The Greek word "metamorphoo" means a complete transformation, like Clark Kent stepping into the phone booth and emerging as Superman, except this was real.

His clothes became dazzling—extremely white as no launderer on earth could whiten them (Mark 9:3). His face shone like the sun. For a brief moment, the ordinary-looking carpenter revealed His true identity: the God of the universe had been walking among them in human skin.

When the Legends Show Up

BUT the story gets crazier. Suddenly Moses and Elijah appear, like having George Washington and Abraham Lincoln materialize to have a conversation. These weren't holograms. The greatest figures from Israel's history showed up to discuss Jesus' mission. Moses, who gave the Law. Elijah, who represented the Prophets. Both pointing to Jesus as the One their entire lives had been preparing the world for. It was like the epic endorsement from history's hall of fame.

Peter's Cringe Moment

LEAVE it to Peter to misread the room. Seeing Jesus talking with these legends, he blurts out, *"Rabbi, it's good for us to be here. Let us put up three shelters: one for you, one for Moses and one for Elijah"* (Mark 9:5).

Peter wanted to turn this into a spiritual Airbnb, treating Jesus like another celebrity alongside Moses and Elijah. But God wasn't having it. A cloud rolled in and the voice from heaven declared, *"This is my beloved Son; listen to him!"* (Mark 9:7).

Then came heaven's finale: *Suddenly, when they looked around, they no longer saw anyone with them except Jesus* (Mark 9:8). Moses gone. Elijah vanished. Only Jesus remained. The message was clear: Stop treating Jesus like one option among many. He's in a category all His own.

Back to Reality

WHAT I love about this story is they couldn't stay on the mountain. Jesus led them back down in Mark 9:9 because real life was waiting. There were people to heal, problems to solve, a world to change. The Christian life isn't meant to be one endless spiritual retreat. We need those moments when

99

God's presence feels tangible, but we also need to bring that power back to our everyday lives where people are struggling and searching.

The Game Changer

THIS transfiguration wasn't just a cool light show for the disciples' Instagram stories. It was a preview of who Jesus really is beneath His humble exterior. When we're tempted to think of Jesus as just another religious teacher or life coach, we need to remember this moment. The same Jesus who got tired and hungry is the one whose glory outshines every star in the universe. That changes how we pray, how we read His words, and how we live our lives.

The next time you're tempted to put your hope in politicians, influencers, or even pastors, remember, they have expiration dates, but Jesus is eternal. The next time you wonder if following Jesus is worth the sacrifice, remember, you're following the one whose glory makes everything look like shadows.

CALL TO ACTION #1: Encounter the extraordinary Jesus. This week, spend time reading the Gospels with fresh eyes. Ask yourself, "Am I treating Jesus like a helpful life coach, or am I recognizing Him as the God of the universe?" Write down one way you can honor His true identity in your daily routine, whether that's how you pray, read Scripture, or talk about Him with others.

CALL TO ACTION #2: Bring mountain power to valley people. God gives us glimpses of His glory not so we can hoard them, but so we can share them. Identify one person in your life who needs to see Jesus' power and love in action. This week, find a practical way to demonstrate His character to that person through forgiveness, generosity, presence in their struggle, or simply sharing your story of who Jesus really is.

42. WiFi Is Full, Still No Internet
~Mark 9:14-29~

"I do believe; help my unbelief!" Mark 9:24 (CSB)

NOTHING is more frustrating than when your phone shows full bars, but nothing works. Everything looks fine, but when it's time to make a call or send a text…silence. The disciples had their own version of this problem in Mark 9. They looked like they had it together spiritually, but when it mattered most, nothing happened.

The Setup for Disaster

JESUS took His inner circle up a mountain for an incredible spiritual experience. But down in the valley, the other nine disciples were facing their worst ministry crisis. A father brought his demon-possessed son for help, and they were completely powerless. Religious leaders stood around watching the failure unfold.

They weren't rookie disciples. Jesus had already given them authority over evil spirits, and they'd cast out demons before. But this time, they accomplished nothing.

The father's words stung: *"I asked your disciples to drive it out, but they couldn't"* (Mark 9:18). Imagine being known as someone who follows Jesus, then having people say your faith doesn't work when it counts.

Jesus Enters the Chaos

WHEN Jesus came down and saw what was happening, He was clearly frustrated. *"You unbelieving generation, how long will I be with you?"* (Mark 9:19).

101

But instead of giving up, Jesus says, "Bring the boy to me." Even when His people fail spectacularly, He doesn't abandon the mission.

The Most Honest Prayer Ever

THE desperate father had just witnessed the disciples fail. So when he approached Jesus, his faith was uncertain. *"If you can do anything, take pity on us and help us" (Mark 9:22).*

Jesus challenged him, *"'If you can?' Everything is possible for the one who believes" (Mark 9:23).*

The father's response is maybe the most honest thing anyone ever said to Jesus, *"I do believe; help my unbelief!"*

He wasn't pretending to have unwavering faith. He was admitting that his belief was mixed with serious doubt. And somehow, that honesty was exactly what Jesus needed.

What Went Wrong

LATER, the disciples asked Jesus privately why they had failed. His answer was simple. *"This kind can come out by nothing but prayer" (Mark 9:29).*

The approach. Instead of pretending we have unshakeable faith, we can be honest about our doubts while still choosing to trust Jesus.

CALL TO ACTION #1: Stop hiding your spiritual struggles behind a perfect image. The father admitted his faith was incomplete, and Jesus worked with that honesty. Bring your real doubts to God instead of performing confidence.

CALL TO ACTION #2: Remember that Jesus is more patient with your growth than you are. The disciples failed completely, but Jesus didn't give up on them. When your faith feels weak, trust that God is still working on you.

43. Spoiler Alert
~Mark 9:30-32~

"The Son of Man is going to be betrayed into the hands of men. They will kill him, and after he is killed, he will rise three days later."
Mark 9:31 (CSB)

WHAT if Marvel dropped the entire plot of the next *Avengers* movie in a 30-second trailer, but everyone watching was like, "Cool action scenes, but what's actually happening?" That's Mark 9:30-32 in a nutshell.

Jesus literally spoiled His own ending—betrayal, death, resurrection—and the disciples were too confused (and too scared) to ask for clarification. Talk about missing the biggest plot twist in history.

The Fear of Looking Dumb

JESUS pulls His disciples aside for some intensive one-on-one teaching time. He's got limited time left (though they don't fully grasp this), and He needs them to understand what's coming. So, He tells them straight up, "The Son of Man is going to be betrayed, killed, and rise again in three days." Their response? Complete confusion and radio silence.

This is like being in math class when everyone's nodding along, but you have absolutely no clue what the teacher just said. The difference? Nobody raised their hand to ask for help.

The Cost of Pride

FEAR of vulnerability kills growth. The disciples were afraid to admit they didn't understand, so they missed out on crucial teaching from Jesus Himself. Think about it. If they had just asked, "Jesus, what do you mean by this?" they might have been better prepared for the crucifixion and resurrection.

Instead, when Jesus was arrested, they were shocked. When He died, they were devastated. When He rose, they were stunned. All because pride kept them from asking the obvious question, "Can you explain that again?"

God wants to train us to be people of faith, not people who need all the answers upfront. Sometimes God tells us what we need to know for the moment, not everything we want to know about the future. Abraham left everything *even though he did not know where he was going (Hebrews 11:8)*. That's the kind of faith that pleases God.

But there's a difference between stepping out in faith and being too proud to ask for clarity when we're genuinely confused.

The Pattern We Still Follow

HOW often do we do this same thing? We sit in church services, small groups, or Bible studies pretending like we understand everything, but inside we're completely lost. We're afraid to raise our hand and say, "I don't get it. Can you break that down for me?"

We'd rather stay confused than risk looking spiritually immature. We'd rather miss out on understanding than admit we need help. Pride becomes the enemy of growth, and our fear of appearing ignorant keeps us actually ignorant.

The disciples' silence in this moment cost them dearly. When the events Jesus predicted actually happened, they were unprepared, scattered, and devastated. Their pride in the moment led to panic in the crisis.

The Beauty of Honest Questions

JESUS never got frustrated with honest questions. He got frustrated with hard hearts, religious hypocrisy, and stubborn unbelief, but never with genuine confusion from people who wanted to understand.

Think about all the times in the Gospels when people asked Jesus to explain His parables, clarify His teachings, or help them understand what He meant. He always responded with patience and additional insight. The problem wasn't asking questions; the problem was being too proud to ask them.

CALL TO ACTION #1: Cancel your comfort subscription and delete your spiritual safety net. Stop trying to follow Jesus while keeping backup plans that prioritize your convenience over His call. This week, identify one area where you've been playing it safe and make the hard choice instead. Unsubscribe from comfortable Christianity and start following the Jesus who demands everything, not just your leftover time and energy.

CALL TO ACTION #2: Practice vulnerable faith. Find where God is calling you to step out in faith, even though you don't have all the answers. Maybe it's starting that ministry, having that difficult conversation, or making that financial commitment. Take one concrete step this week, trusting that God will provide clarity as you move forward.

The disciples were close to understanding because they grasped the concepts but hadn't crossed the line into honest inquiry. Don't let pride rob you of the growth God wants to give you. Sometimes the most spiritual thing you can do is admit you don't have it all figured out.

44. Why Being Last Makes You First
~Mark 9:33-37~

Sitting down, he called the Twelve and said to them, "If anyone wants to be first, he must be last and servant of all." Mark 9:35 (CSB)

LINKEDIN feeds are full of people flexing their promotions, new cars, and "hustle culture" wins. Meanwhile, Jesus drops the most counterintuitive career advice ever: "Want to be first? Be last. Want to be great? Serve everyone."

This would definitely break the internet.

The Disciples' Group Chat Drama

IN Mark 9:33-37, the disciples were basically having their own version of a heated group chat argument, except it was face-to-face and about who was the GOAT among them. Sound familiar? We've all been there, whether it's comparing follower counts, salaries, or achievements.

When Jesus caught wind of their debate, He didn't give them a motivational speech about grinding harder. Instead, He grabbed a little kid (someone with zero social status, no blue checkmark, no influence) and said, "This is your role model."

The Awkward Silence

CAN you imagine the awkwardness? These grown men had just been arguing about their spiritual rankings, and Jesus responds by putting a child in the center of their circle. In the first-century, children had no social standing, no legal rights, and no voice in important matters. It's as if they were invisible.

But Jesus said, *"Whoever welcomes one little child such as this in my name welcomes me. And whoever welcomes me does not welcome me, but him who sent me" (Mark 9:37)*. He was essentially saying, "If you want to know how great you are in God's kingdom, look at how you treat the people who can't do anything for you."

Service Over Status: The Real Flex

ACCORDING to Jesus, greatness values service over status. While there's nothing wrong with ambition or working toward goals, the trap comes when status makes us think the world revolves around us. Jesus flipped the script: true greatness isn't about elevating yourself; it's about having a "you first" mentality through humility.

The disciples were thinking like the world thinks: greatness means being served, having people cater to your needs, being recognized and honored. Jesus introduced a completely different metric: greatness means serving others, especially those who can't repay you.

The Child Standard

WHY did Jesus use a child as His example? Because children represent the powerless, the overlooked, the ones who need care rather than offering advantage. While we are preoccupied with networking and leveraging relationships for personal gain, Jesus said true greatness is measured by how you treat people who can't help your career.

When you welcome a child, you're not making a strategic move. You're not building your brand or expanding your influence. You're simply showing love to someone who needs it. That's the heart of kingdom greatness.

The Upside-Down Kingdom

EVERYTHING about God's kingdom operates on different principles than the world's system. The world says climb the ladder, step on others if necessary, and make sure you get yours. Jesus says the ladder is upside-down—the way up is down, the way to lead is to serve, the way to be great is to be humble.

This doesn't mean being a doormat or having no ambition. It means redefining success according to God's standards rather than culture's metrics. It means finding fulfillment in making others successful rather than just promoting yourself.

CALL TO ACTION #1: Take the 24-hour service challenge. For the next 24 hours, intentionally put someone else's needs before your own convenience. Hold the elevator, buy coffee for the person behind you, or simply listen without trying to one-up their story. Look for opportunities to serve without any possibility of recognition or reward.

CALL TO ACTION #2: Adopt a "forgotten" person. Identify someone in your circle who feels overlooked. Maybe it's the new person at work, an elderly neighbor, or someone going through a tough time. Reach out this week with a text, call, or coffee invitation. Make them feel seen and valued. Don't do it for the story or the social media post; do it because Jesus said welcoming the overlooked is the same as welcoming Him.

True greatness isn't about climbing the ladder; it's about helping others up. In God's economy, the last shall be first, and the servants shall be the greatest.

45. Don't Fight Your Teammates
~Mark 9:38-41~

"Whoever is not against us is for us." Mark 9:40 (CSB)

AT a high school basketball game, I saw something wild. Two players from the same team got into an argument on the court. One threw a punch. Coaches and players rushed in to break it up. I just sat there thinking, "Why would you fight your teammate when the real opponent is in front of you?" That moment came to mind while reading Mark 9. The disciples tried to shut someone down not because he was doing wrong, but because he wasn't part of their group. And the person they tried to stop was doing the very thing they had failed to do.

A Narrow Perspective

JOHN tells Jesus, *"We saw someone driving out demons in your name, and we tried to stop him because he wasn't following us"* (Mark 9:38). He thought he was protecting Jesus' reputation, but Jesus didn't see it that way. Instead of agreeing, Jesus responds, *"Don't stop him, because there is no one who will perform a miracle in my name who can soon afterward speak evil of me. For whoever is not against us is for us"* (Mark 9:39-40). Jesus reminds them that the kingdom of God can't be boxed in by group labels. The goal is not to guard a brand but to glorify the King.

Small Acts, Big Impacts

JESUS goes further. Even giving a cup of water to someone because they belong to Him will be rewarded. God notices what others overlook. While the disciples were trying to control who counted, Jesus was honoring even the smallest act done in His name.

The Real Struggle

THIS wasn't about the outsider. It was about the disciples' pride. They were more focused on ownership than impact. It's easy to fall into that mindset today. We criticize other churches or leaders not because they are wrong, but because they are not part of our crew. We care more about recognition than results.

The Bigger Picture

WE are called to unity. The real enemy is not the believer down the street with a different method. It is the darkness stealing hope from people who need the gospel. Let's stop wasting energy competing with our teammates. There is more than enough work and reward for everyone who follows Christ.

CALL TO ACTION #1: Check your heart posture. This week, pay attention to your reactions when you see other people or churches experiencing success. Do you feel joy, or are you critical because they're not "your people"? Ask God to reveal pride or territorial spirit in your heart. Then celebrate one ministry or leader this week who's doing kingdom work differently than you would.

CALL TO ACTION #2: Offer your "cup of water." Jesus says giving someone a cup of water in His name matters. Find one way this week to encourage someone in your community—a neighbor, coworker, or even a stranger. It could be a kind word, practical help, or simply being present when someone needs it.

46. Jesus Canceled "Meek And Mild"
~Mark 9:42-50~

"And if your hand causes you to fall away, cut it off."
Mark 9:43 (CSB)

IF Jesus had a marketing team today, they'd probably red pen Mark 9:42-50. Too edgy for the target audience. Too much truth for a generation conditioned to hear only grace. But Jesus never paid consultants to make Him palatable, and the result is some of the most difficult teaching He ever gave.

Just as Jesus finished speaking about safeguarding little ones from stumbling, He swerves. Hard. Before you know it, He's speaking about millstones and amputations and outer darkness. This isn't Jesus in a bad mood. This is Jesus loving us enough to say what's at stake.

Sin is not a problem to be managed. It's not a nuisance to be accommodated. It's cancer, and it will kill you if you don't cut it out. Jesus is not holding back because He values your comfort. Eternity is at stake. He would rather jolt you awake than let you sleepwalk into hell.

When Jesus speaks about cutting off hands and plucking out eyes, He's speaking in intentional hyperbole to a culture fluent in the language of symbols. The Jewish rabbis of Jesus' day understood the hand symbolized action, the foot symbolized direction, and the eye symbolized desire.

In essence, what Jesus is saying is this: If your hand causes you to fall away, cut it off. Your actions are leading you into sin. Cut them out. If your foot causes you to stumble, cut it off. The direction of your life is leading you

111

into sin. Change course. If your eye causes you to sin, pluck it out. Your desires are leading you into sin. Tear them out.

The Jewish rabbis understood this was figurative language. Literally cutting off your hand does nothing to your heart's capacity to do evil. A blind person can still lust. A handless person can still think murderous thoughts. Jesus is calling for spiritual amputation, not literal self-harm.

But let's not let the metaphorical nature make this sound less shocking. Jesus is calling us to take sin so seriously that we're willing to make painful cuts. That relationship pulling you away from God? That habit corrupting your witness? That media defiling your mind? Whatever it is, Jesus says better to lose that than lose your soul.

Jesus will certainly make your life better in a hundred ways. But if you're only expecting Him to buff up your existing priorities, you're in for a shock. He's not an upgrade package. He's a complete reconstruction.

Jesus concludes with images of salt and fire. We will all go through fire. Some will experience the refining fire that purges selfishness and pride. Others will endure the final fire of judgment. God's refining fire is not comfortable, but it is good. It burns away everything false and leaves behind something real. When you let Him purify you, you become salt in a flavorless world.

CALL TO ACTION #1: Stop bargaining with God. Identify one thing you know needs to go but you keep making excuses to keep. Cut it off this week and trust God to replace what He removes with something better.

CALL TO ACTION #2: Choose the difficult path. Jesus called the disciples to die to themselves completely. What area are you still holding back? Stop playing it safe and follow Him.

47. Marriage: Vintage Vibes
~Mark 10:1-12~

But from the beginning of creation God made them male and female. For this reason a man will leave his father and mother and the two will become one flesh. So they are no longer two, but one flesh. Therefore what God has joined together, let no one separate.
Mark 10:6-9 (CSB)

God's Original Design vs. Our Broken Reality

NOWADAYS everyone is redefining everything—gender, marriage, family, even basic biology. It's like we're playing a massive game of "make your own rules" and then getting mad when other people don't follow our personal rulebook. But what if the original Designer actually knew what He was doing when He created the blueprint for human relationships?

The Pharisees' Gotcha Question

THE Pharisees thought they had Jesus cornered with a controversial question about divorce. But Jesus didn't get caught up in their legal loopholes. Instead, He went back to the source code of Genesis 1 and 2, God's original design for marriage.

"From the beginning of creation God made them male and female," Jesus said, quoting Genesis 1:27. This wasn't just a biology lesson; it was a theology lesson. God intentionally created two distinct, complementary genders that would come together in marriage to reflect His image.

The Divine Blueprint

WHEN God said, *"Let us make man in our image" (Genesis 1:26)*, He created them *male and female (Genesis 1:27)*. The image of God isn't fully expressed in one gender alone. It takes both masculine and feminine, working together in covenant relationship, to reflect the fullness of God's character.

This is why Jesus points to Genesis 2:24: *A man leaves his father and mother and bonds with his wife, and they become one flesh*. This isn't just about sexual union; it's about two distinct but complementary beings becoming a new, unified entity that displays God's design for relationship.

More Than Just Preference

MARRIAGE has become about personal happiness, romantic feelings, and individual fulfillment. But God's design for marriage between a man and a woman goes deeper than preference. It's about purpose. It's about reflecting the relationship between Christ and the church (Ephesians 5:32). It's about creating the optimal environment for raising the next generation. It's about displaying God's character within complementary differences.

The Complementary Design

MEN and women aren't identical. That's not a bug in the system. It's a feature. We bring different strengths, perspectives, and gifts to the relationship. When a man and woman come together in marriage, they create something that neither could create alone—a partnership that reflects both the strength and tenderness, the justice and mercy, the leadership and nurture that characterize God Himself.

The Cultural Pushback

I KNOW this isn't popular. In a social climate that insists "love is love" and "marriage equality," standing for God's original design feels like swimming upstream. But truth isn't determined by popular vote or cultural trends. God's design for marriage isn't about limiting love; it's about defining the context where love can flourish according to His plan.

The Heart Behind the Design

GOD didn't create marriage between a man and a woman to be restrictive. He created it to be restorative. In a world broken by sin, marriage becomes an example of covenant love, sacrificial commitment, and the kind of relationship God wants with us. When we follow His design, we experience the fullness of what He intended.

CALL TO ACTION #1: Celebrate God's design. In our social climate, believing in biblical marriage feels like you need to apologize or whisper it quietly. But God's design for marriage isn't something to be ashamed of. It's something to celebrate and defend with grace and truth. This week, find one opportunity to speak positively about God's design for marriage. Don't just argue against what you oppose; advocate for what God supports. Share why complementary marriage is beautiful, not just why alternatives fall short.

CALL TO ACTION #2: Live out the design so well that others want what you have. The best case for biblical marriage isn't a theological debate; it's a thriving relationship that makes others want what you have. If you're married, commit to one specific way you'll honor your spouse and display complementary partnership. If you're single, prepare yourself to enter God's design for marriage with wisdom and maturity. Let your life be such a compelling picture of God's design that it draws others to His truth.

48. Kiddie Faith Is Your Superpower
~Mark 10:13-16~

"Truly I tell you, whoever does not receive the kingdom of God like a little child will never enter it." Mark 10:15 (CSB)

AT networking events, the most successful person is usually surrounded by important people trying to get their attention. Not exactly the time or place for a bunch of kids to show off their drawings to an influencer. Most adults would shoo the kids away, "Can't you see we're having important conversations here?"

But Jesus? He got angry at the adults and welcomed the children.

The Disciples' Epic Fail

THE disciples thought they were being helpful by protecting Jesus from interruption. After all, He was doing important ministry work—teaching, healing, changing lives. Surely He didn't have time for kids who just wanted attention.

But Jesus was *indignant* (that's biblical language for "seriously ticked off"). He didn't just tolerate the children; He held them up as the gold standard for entering God's kingdom.

What Kids Get That Adults Miss

CHILDREN approach life with qualities that adults often lose: complete trust, unfiltered wonder, total dependence, and zero pretense. They don't try to earn love; they just receive it. They don't overthink gifts; they just enjoy them. They don't worry about looking foolish; they just believe.

116

Jesus is saying that all our adult sophistication, our theological degrees, our spiritual résumés mean nothing if we've lost the simple ability to trust like a child. The kingdom of God isn't for people who have it all figured out; it's for people who know they need help.

The Humility Revolution

IN our achievement-obsessed mindset, this is revolutionary. We're taught to be self-sufficient, to earn our way, to prove our worth. But Jesus says the people closest to God's heart are those who approach Him with empty hands and open hearts.

Children don't bring anything to the table except need and trust. They don't negotiate terms or try to impress anyone. They just run to the person they love and believe that person will take care of them.

CALL TO ACTION #1: Recover your wonder. Ask God one question you've always wondered about but felt too "mature" to ask. Find a pastor or mentor and discuss.

CALL TO ACTION #2: Pass the faith forward. Jesus was indignant when adults tried to keep children away from Him. How are you treating the children in your church and community? This week, find one specific way to bless, encourage, or invest in a child. Volunteer in children's ministry, mentor a young person, or simply take time to really listen to a kid in your life. Show them the same welcome that Jesus showed.

49. The Million-Dollar Question
~Mark 10:17-31~

*Looking at him, Jesus loved him and said to him, "You lack one thing:
Go, sell all you have and give to the poor, and you will have treasure
in heaven. Then come, follow me." Mark 10:21 (CSB)*

SOMETIMES the things we believe will fulfill us are the very
things that enslave us. A dream job becomes overly
stressful. A perfect relationship grows unhealthy. Financial
security starts to control us instead of freeing us. That is
exactly where the rich young ruler found himself. He had
everything he thought he needed, yet something was
missing.

This man was wealthy, respected, morally upright, and
spiritually curious. He had kept the commandments since
his youth. He was the kind of person churches would
spotlight in their newsletters. His life looked like the
American dream wrapped in religious devotion.

But Jesus saw what others missed. His wealth had
quietly taken God's place. It gave him identity, comfort, and
control over his circumstances. It was not just something he
had accumulated. It had him completely. Every decision was
filtered through how it would affect his financial standing
and social status.

Mark gives us a powerful detail that reveals Jesus'
heart: *Looking at him, Jesus loved him.* What Jesus said next was
not a harsh demand or spiritual test. It was a loving
challenge designed to heal this man's soul and expose the
idol he was worshiping.

The Son of God does not ask every person to sell
everything. This was not a one-size-fits-all command. It was
personal and surgical, tailored for this individual. Jesus

118

identified what was holding this man back from trusting God. His possessions had become his real god, his source of security.

The man went away grieving. Not because Jesus was cruel, but because he could not let go of what controlled him. He chose temporary security over eternal life. He walked away from the greatest opportunity in human history because the cost felt too high.

Jesus turned to His disciples and said, *"How hard it is for those who have wealth to enter the kingdom of God!" (Mark 10:23).* Not because money is bad, but because it gives the illusion of self-sufficiency. Wealth whispers lies about our ability to control destiny.

The disciples were stunned. If this man could not be saved, who could? Jesus answered, *"With man it is impossible, but not with God, because all things are possible with God" (Mark 10:27).*

This is not about giving all away. It is about trusting God above all.

CALL TO ACTION #1: Identify your functional god.
What would be hardest for you to surrender if Jesus asked? Probably where your trust lies. Confess it and invite God to take His rightful place.

CALL TO ACTION #2: Practice radical generosity.
Find one way to give sacrificially this week. Trust that God sees and will reward what you release.

50. How Jesus Flips The Success Script
~Mark 10:32-45~

They answered him, "Allow us to sit at your right and at your left in your glory." Mark 10:37 (CSB)

MODERN society is obsessed with influence and image. People chase likes, build brands, and fight to be first. Leadership books and social media feeds tell us to climb higher, hustle harder, and make ourselves known. But Jesus offers a completely different version of success.

In Mark 10, Jesus is walking toward Jerusalem. He knows what is coming—betrayal, suffering, and death. Meanwhile, His disciples are caught up in a conversation about power and prestige. James and John ask Jesus for the most honored seats in His kingdom. It is like asking for the corner office while the company is burning to the ground.

What happens next should make every follower of Jesus pause. Jesus does not scold them. He questions them. *"Are you able to drink the cup I drink?"* (Mark 10:38). The cup represents His suffering. The path they are asking to walk is not paved with recognition. It is paved with sacrifice.

Then Jesus redefines greatness. While the world seeks to climb, He calls His followers to serve. While others reach for influence, He invites His disciples to take the lowest position. He says, *"Whoever wants to become great among you will be your servant, and whoever wants to be first among you will be a slave to all"* (Mark 10:42-44). That is not just a leadership principle. That is the heartbeat of Jesus Himself.

He continues, *"For even the Son of Man did not come to be served, but to serve, and to give his life as a ransom for many"* (Mark 10:45). True greatness is not about titles or recognition. It is about laying down your life for others. The disciples were looking for glory, but Jesus was modeling the way of the cross. He wasn't just teaching servanthood—He was living it out in real time. While they dreamed of thrones, He was already preparing to wash feet. His leadership style was radical because it prioritized others over self, sacrifice over comfort, and love over recognition.

CALL TO ACTION #1: Shift from consumer to contributor. James and John were focused on what they could gain. But Jesus modeled a life of giving. Ask yourself, "Am I approaching God to receive, or am I responding to His love by serving others?" Look for ways this week to meet a need without expecting anything in return.

CALL TO ACTION #2: Serve where you are, not where you hope to be. You do not need a platform or a title to make a difference. You just need a heart like Jesus. Start by loving the people around you. Encourage someone. Help a neighbor. Support a friend. Look for the towel, not the throne.

The world says to be seen. Jesus says to see others. True greatness is not measured by how high you climb but by how low you are willing to go to lift others up.

51. Blind Faith, Clear Vision
~Mark 10:46-52~

They came to Jericho. And as he was leaving Jericho with his disciples and a large crowd, Bartimaeus (the son of Timaeus), a blind beggar, was sitting by the road. Mark 10:46 (CSB)

SOME moments in life demand that you stop surviving and start shouting.

In this day and age, people carefully manage their image and hold tightly to whatever gives them a sense of control. But what happens when Jesus calls you to leave behind the very thing that has defined you? Sometimes the objects we cling to most are the ones keeping us stuck.

Enter Bartimaeus. He is blind. He is poor. And he is stuck on the side of the road in Jericho. But when he hears that Jesus is nearby, something stirs in him. This is not just a popular figure passing through. Bartimaeus has heard the stories. He believes Jesus has the power to heal.

The Bold Cry

WHILE others crowd around hoping for a glimpse, Bartimaeus begins shouting from the roadside. *"Jesus, Son of David, have mercy on me!" (Mark 10:47)*. He is loud. He is persistent. People try to quiet him, but he refuses to be silenced.

What is striking is that Bartimaeus, though physically blind, has spiritual clarity. He calls Jesus by His messianic title, Son of David. He recognizes the identity that the crowd cannot see.

The Personal Question

JESUS hears the cry and stops. In the middle of the noise and the people, He singles out one man and asks, *"What do you want me to do for you?" (Mark 10:51)*.

Jesus does not assume. He invites Bartimaeus to name his need. That same question echoes to you today. If Jesus asked you that right now, how would you respond?

The Defining Moment

BARTIMAEUS wastes no time. He springs up and leaves behind his only possession. His outer garment likely served as his shelter and symbol of his status as a beggar. Yet he lets it go without hesitation. He chooses the unknown with Jesus over the familiar life he has always known.

The New Road

ONCE healed, Bartimaeus does not celebrate and return to his old spot. He joins Jesus on the road. That path leads to Jerusalem. That road leads to the cross. Bartimaeus follows Jesus into the very heart of the gospel story.

CALL TO ACTION #1: Name what you need to release. What do you cling to that gives you false security? Is it your image, comfort, control, or past? Jesus calls you to leave it behind and come to Him fully.

CALL TO ACTION #2: Follow without delay. Bartimaeus did not settle for healing alone. He followed Jesus. Move from receiving to responding. Walk the road with Him, even when the journey costs more than you expected.

52. Super Flex
~Mark 11:1-11~

When they approached Jerusalem, at Bethphage and Bethany near the Mount of Olives, he sent two of his disciples and told them, "Go into the village ahead of you. As soon as you enter it, you will find a colt tied there, on which no one has ever sat. Untie it and bring it."
Mark 11:1-2 (CSB)

WHAT if you got a message that said, "God needs you for something today"? Would you treat it like any other notification and move on, or would you drop everything and say, "I'm ready. Let's go"?

Your Creator Says, "I Need You"

MARK 11:1-11 drops one of the most mind-blowing phrases in Scripture: *"The Lord needs it."* Think about that for a second. The God who spoke galaxies into existence, who holds the ocean in His palm, who never sleeps or gets tired—He has need of something. Not just anything, but specifically what you have to offer.

Jesus sent His disciples to get a colt with the simplest explanation ever: *"The Lord needs it."* No lengthy justification, no detailed business plan, just a straightforward truth. And the kicker—when the disciples said those exact words to the owners, they immediately let the colt go. Something about knowing God had a specific need unlocked their generosity instantly.

The colt had never been ridden, never been "useful" in the traditional sense. Yet this was the exact moment it was born for: to carry the King of kings into Jerusalem. Its whole existence led to this one divine appointment.

But what hits different: after the triumphant entry, after all the "Hosannas" and palm branches, Jesus simply looked around and left because it was evening (Mark 11:11). The colt's moment of glory was brief, but it was eternal in significance.

CALL TO ACTION #1: Stop underestimating your "ordinary." Your everyday availability is God's extraordinary opportunity. That colt wasn't special until Jesus needed it. Your job, your apartment, your car, your skills, your story—they might seem ordinary to you, but they're exactly what God wants to use. Stop waiting to feel "qualified" or "ready." The Lord has need of you right now, exactly as you are. Your willingness matters more than your worthiness.

CALL TO ACTION #2: Practice the "say less" response. When God calls, don't negotiate—participate. The colt's owners didn't ask for references, demand a deposit, or require a detailed explanation. They heard, *"The Lord needs it,"* and immediately released what they had. What would change in your life if you responded to God's nudges with that same instant obedience? When you feel prompted, encourage someone, serve somewhere, or step up somehow. Say less; do more.

The same Jesus who needed a donkey for His Jerusalem entrance needs you for His kingdom work today. He's not looking for perfect people; He's looking for available people. The question isn't whether you're good enough; it's whether you're willing enough.

Your moment might be brief, but its impact can be eternal. The Lord has need of you.

53. Beautiful Walls, Broken Pipes
~Mark 11:12-26~

The next day when they went out from Bethany, he was hungry. Seeing in the distance a fig tree with leaves, he went to find out if there was anything on it. When he came to it, he found nothing but leaves; for it was not the season for figs. He said to it, "May no one ever eat fruit from you again!" And his disciples heard it. Mark 11:12-14 (CSB)

MY neighbor's house looks incredible from the street. Perfect lawn, fresh paint, those expensive shutters that make everyone slow down when they drive by. Last month, new owners discovered the foundation was cracked, electrical hadn't been updated since the 1970s, and mold was behind every wall. All that money spent on curb appeal, but nothing worked.

Jesus found something similar with the fig tree.

The False Advertisement

FIG trees in that region would sprout small, edible buds before the leaves appeared. A tree covered in leaves was advertising: "Fresh figs here!" This tree looked healthy and productive from a distance. Up close, it advertised something it couldn't deliver. Jesus was hungry. He approached, expecting nourishment, and found nothing but empty promises wrapped in beautiful foliage. The tree had mastered appearance but failed at its purpose.

When God Inspects

GOD doesn't drive by and admire our spiritual landscaping. He walks to the front door and looks inside. He examines the foundation, not just the paint we've applied for Sunday morning.

Pride grows quietly behind well-maintained exteriors. Bitterness spreads through walls while we're busy polishing our public image. Selfishness corrodes the infrastructure while everyone compliments our spiritual decorating. Sometimes these hidden problems develop over years. By the time they're visible, they've already compromised everything we've built.

The Hard Choice

THE fig tree had reached a point where cosmetic fixes wouldn't help. Jesus wasn't being cruel when He cursed it. Sometimes structures need to be condemned so something healthy can replace them. God's Word acts like an inspector, revealing problems we might not know exist. This isn't meant to crush us, but to help us address issues before they cause damage. Most spiritual lives aren't beyond repair. God specializes in restoration projects others abandon. He can rebuild foundations, rewire systems, and restore what seems hopeless.

CALL TO ACTION #1: Stop focusing on spiritual curb appeal and start examining the foundation. Ask God to reveal problems that need attention before they cause major damage.

CALL TO ACTION #2: Invest in infrastructure that actually produces spiritual fruit rather than just improving appearances. Strengthen disciplines and address character issues that matter more than appearances.

Beautiful leaves catch attention, but fruit feeds people. What really matters is whether faith works when God looks for nourishment.

54. Getting Schooled
~Mark 11:27-33~

They came again to Jerusalem. As he was walking in the temple, the chief priests, the scribes, and the elders came and asked him, "By what authority are you doing these things? Who gave you this authority to do these things?" Mark 11:27-28 (CSB)

WHEN someone tries to outsmart you with a question, but you turn the tables and leave them speechless—that's exactly what happened when the religious elite tried to corner Jesus in the temple courts.

The chief priests, scribes, and elders thought they had Jesus trapped. They rolled up with their credentials, their religious authority, and their carefully crafted question designed to destroy His ministry. *"By what authority are you doing these things?"* they demanded, expecting Him to either claim divine authority (which they could call blasphemy) or admit He had no authority at all.

But Jesus wasn't playing their game.

The Master Class Response

INSTEAD of walking into their trap, Jesus responded with His own question: *"I will ask you one question; then answer me, and I will tell you by what authority I do these things. Was John's baptism from heaven or of human origin? Answer me" (Mark 11:29-30).*

Brilliant. With one question, Jesus exposed their hypocrisy and put them in an impossible position. If they said John's baptism was from heaven, Jesus would ask why they didn't believe him when John pointed to Jesus as the Messiah. If they said it was merely human, the crowd would turn against them because everyone believed John was a prophet.

The Silence of Defeat

THE religious leaders huddled together like a football team calling a timeout, desperately trying to find a way out of the corner they'd painted themselves into. Finally, they admitted defeat: *"We don't know" (Mark 11:33).*

Jesus responded with the verbal equivalent of a mic drop, *"Neither will I tell you by what authority I do these things" (Mark 11:33).*

The Authority Question

THE irony is thick here. These men were questioning the authority of the One who created authority itself. They were challenging the credentials of the God who gave them their positions in the first place. They were demanding proof from the One who was proof incarnate.

Their question revealed their real problem. They weren't genuinely seeking truth. They were protecting their turf. They weren't interested in Jesus' authority because they were threatened by it. His authority exposed their lack of it.

The Modern Classroom

THIS same dynamic plays out today. People challenge Jesus' authority not because they genuinely want answers, but because they want to maintain control of their own lives. They ask questions not to learn, but to avoid surrendering.

The religious leaders thought they were the teachers, but they became the students. They thought they were examining Jesus, but He was examining them. They thought they were in control, but they were completely outmaneuvered.

129

The Heart Behind the Question

JESUS didn't answer their question because He knew their hearts. They weren't asking because they wanted to follow Him if He proved His authority. They were asking because they wanted to trap Him regardless of His answer.

God doesn't owe skeptics proof when their skepticism is really rebellion in disguise. He doesn't need to defend His authority to people who have already decided to reject it.

The Authority We All Face

THE question these religious leaders asked is one we all must answer: Will we submit to Jesus' authority or challenge it? Will we recognize His right to rule our lives, or will we keep trying to maintain control?

The difference between genuine seekers and religious game-players is this: seekers ask questions because they want to know the truth. Game-players ask questions because they want to avoid the truth.

CALL TO ACTION #1: Examine your motives when you question God's ways. Are you genuinely seeking understanding, or are you trying to maintain control? This week, identify one area where you've been challenging God's authority instead of submitting to it. Choose surrender over skepticism.

CALL TO ACTION #2: Recognize Jesus' authority in your daily decisions instead of compartmentalizing your faith. Let His lordship influence your relationships, finances, career choices, and priorities. Ask yourself, "Am I living like Jesus has authority over this area of my life, or am I still trying to be the boss?"

55. Squatters' Rights
~Mark 12:1-12~

"What then will the owner of the vineyard do? He will come and kill the farmers and give the vineyard to others." Mark 12:9 (CSB)

A FEW years ago, I sold a rental property. Upon closing, the new owners discovered there was an anonymous person living in the unit. The new family was ready to move in, but the squatter replied, "I need more time to find a new place to live. Can you give me an extra week?" Can you believe that someone who was living rent-free and unauthorized had the audacity to ask for "more time"? He actually expected the owner to come back later.

Turns out, we've all mastered the art of claiming what isn't ours. From "manifesting" our dream life to "speaking things into existence," we've convinced ourselves we deserve whatever we want. Somewhere along the way, we became spiritual squatters who move into God's blessings, set up camp in His grace, and act shocked when He reminds us who actually holds the deed.

The Original Squatters

JESUS tells the story of vineyard workers who started as tenants but ended up as squatters. The owner leased them his property and went away, expecting his share of the harvest. But these workers forgot they were renters, not owners. When the landlord sent servants to collect what was his, the squatters got violent. They beat one, stoned another, and killed a third. These weren't bad tenants; they were criminals claiming squatters' rights through intimidation and murder.

131

The vineyard owner represents God, the tenants represent Israel's religious leaders, and the servants represent the prophets God sent. Each time God sent a messenger to call His people back, they rejected, persecuted, or killed them.

The Heir Gets the Eviction Notice

FINALLY, the owner sends his beloved son, thinking surely they'll respect the heir. But the squatters see this as their chance to make their illegal occupation permanent: *"This is the heir! Let's kill him, and the inheritance will be ours!"* *(Mark 12:7)*. Squatters' logic completely breaks down. They thought murdering the heir would give them legal claim to the property. Instead, it guaranteed their eviction and destruction.

This is exactly what the religious leaders were planning to do with Jesus. They saw Him as a threat to their authority and were plotting His death, thinking they could eliminate God's claim on their lives.

No Squatters' Rights in God's Kingdom

THE religious leaders got the message. They'd been squatting in God's vineyard (Israel), treating it like their property instead of stewarding it for the true Owner. They'd rejected God's messengers and were about to kill His Son, thinking they could claim ownership of what was never theirs. But Jesus delivers the eviction notice with Psalm 118: *"The stone that the builders rejected has become the cornerstone"* *(Mark 12:10)*. The one they were rejecting would become the foundation of God's new building, and their squatters' rights would be permanently revoked.

Your Spiritual Lease Agreement

THE uncomfortable truth is we're all tenants, not owners. Your life, your talents, your family, your resources—you're managing God's property, not claiming squatters' rights. The moment you act like you own what belongs to God, you become a spiritual squatter headed for eviction. God entrusts us with His blessings not so we can hoard them, but so we can steward them. When He sends correction or calls for accountability, our response reveals whether we see ourselves as grateful tenants or entitled squatters.

The Choice Before Us

THE vineyard will be given to others, to those who produce fruit and honor the Owner. God is looking for faithful stewards who remember their place and fulfill their responsibilities.

CALL TO ACTION #1: Embrace your tenant status. Live as a grateful steward instead of acting like you own what belongs to God. Are you treating your life like you have squatters' rights to God's blessings? Check your lease agreement with heaven. Everything you have is entrusted to you by God, not owned by you.

CALL TO ACTION #2: Surrender to God's correction. Receive His discipline as love instead of rejecting it as interference. The vineyard workers killed the messengers because they didn't want accountability to the owner. What areas of your life are you protecting from God's input? Where are you silencing His voice because you prefer your own way? Welcome His correction as evidence of His care. In God's kingdom, there are no squatters' rights, only grateful tenants and foolish trespassers. Which one are you?

56. The Face That You're Showing
~Mark 12:13-17~

Then they sent some of the Pharisees and the Herodians to Jesus to trap him in his words. "Is it lawful to pay taxes to Caesar or not? Should we pay or shouldn't we?" Mark 12:14 (CSB)

THINK about the last time you wore your favorite brand. Maybe it was Nike, Carhartt, or something vintage you picked up at a thrift store. That logo says something about you—what you like, what you support, maybe even what tribe you belong to. But what if someone asked, "Whose image are you wearing, not just on your jacket, but in the way you live your life?"

A group of religious and political leaders try to trap Jesus with a tricky question about taxes. They want Him to either oppose Caesar and get in trouble with Rome, or side with Caesar and lose credibility with the people. Either way, they think they've cornered Him.

Jesus doesn't take the bait. He asks for a coin and points out Caesar's face on it. Then He says, *"Give to Caesar the things that are Caesar's, and to God the things that are God's (Mark 12:17).*

Jesus doesn't just answer their question; He reframes it. He shifts their focus from politics to purpose, from temporary systems to eternal truths. If the coin belongs to Caesar because it bears his image, then what belongs to God? What carries His image? You do. I do. We all do. That one statement speaks volumes.

From the beginning, Genesis 1:27 says that God created humans in His own image. That means we carry His likeness—not physically, but in our capacity to think, create, choose love, pursue justice, and live with purpose. You're not just someone scrolling through life. You're a walking reflection of the One who made you. You were designed to reveal something divine.

The world is always handing out labels. People will try to define you by your popularity, your performance, your past. But none of that determines your identity. You belong to God. His image is already on you. The only question is, are you reflecting Him clearly?

CALL TO ACTION #1: Reclaim your identity. Stop letting social pressure or insecurity write your story. You are made in the image of God. That's where your worth comes from. Let that shape how you see yourself and how you move through your day. It's not something you earn; it's already true. You don't have to hustle for what's already been stamped on your soul.

CALL TO ACTION #2: Represent God with bold intention. If His image is stamped on your life, let it show with purpose. Don't blend in just to survive. Stand out to reflect who you belong to. Let your creativity carry His fingerprints. Let your compassion disrupt someone's bad day. Let your choices point to something deeper than self. You're not here to coast—you're here to shine. Every decision, every word, every moment is a chance to mirror your Maker.

57. Fact-Checked By Jesus
~Mark 12:18-27~

"Isn't this the reason why you're mistaken: you don't know the Scriptures or the power of God?" Mark 12:24 (CSB)

THE Sadducees thought they had the perfect "gotcha" question for Jesus—like trying to stump Google with a riddle, only to discover they'd been using Internet Explorer their whole lives.

Mark gives us one of the boldest theological corrections in the Bible. The Sadducees, who didn't even believe in resurrection, approached Jesus with a hypothetical story meant to trap Him: a woman who'd been married to seven brothers. Their question? "Whose wife will she be in the resurrection?" It was dripping with cynicism, like saying, "If heaven existed (which we don't think it does), wouldn't it be ridiculous?"

But Jesus didn't just answer the question; He pulled back the curtain on their entire belief system. *"Isn't this the reason why you're mistaken?"* He said. *"You don't know the Scriptures or the power of God."* (Mark 12:24) Translation: You're not just off; you're confidently off.

The religious elite walked into what they assumed would be an easy debate, only to get completely deconstructed by the carpenter from Nazareth. It's like showing up to a chess match and realizing your opponent has been playing 4D chess while you're still learning checkers. The Sadducees had built their entire theology around what they could see and control, but Jesus operated from an entirely different operating system—one that included resurrection, eternal life, and the unlimited power of God. Their approach was like trying to understand the internet using a flip phone. They had the right intentions but completely outdated software.

Then Jesus brought them back to the part of Scripture they did trust: Moses and the burning bush. God had told Moses, *"I am the God of Abraham, Isaac, and Jacob" (Mark 12:26)*. Not was… *am*. That one verb crushed their argument. God isn't the God of the dead, He's the God of the living. Abraham, Isaac, and Jacob weren't gone; they were still alive in God's presence, awaiting resurrection.

And then Jesus added something many didn't expect: there's no marriage in the resurrection. People will be like angels, not in appearance but in nature: fully alive, completely fulfilled, and eternally connected to God. Rather than losing love, we'll gain something deeper. The most meaningful relationship on earth is just a preview of the closeness we'll experience with our Creator.

CALL TO ACTION #1: Check your spiritual blind spots.
The Sadducees were devout and educated, but they had stopped learning. What assumptions are you carrying about God that might need to be reexamined? Ask Him to search your heart. Stay teachable. Study Scripture like it still has something new to show you—because it does.

CALL TO ACTION #2: Enlarge your vision of God's power.
The Sadducees made the mistake of thinking God was limited by human logic. Don't do the same. God's plans aren't just smarter; they're in an entirely different category. Resurrection isn't a side note; it's central. His power doesn't just restore; it recreates.

Let Jesus challenge your assumptions. Let truth break through the fog. Let resurrection hope shape how you live today.

58. The Ultimate Cheat Code
~Mark 12:28-34~

One of the scribes approached. When he heard them debating and saw that Jesus answered them well, he asked him, "Which command is the most important of all?" Mark 12:28 (CSB)

AMIDST endless life hacks, productivity tools, and motivational formulas, Jesus gave the cheat code for how to live with purpose: two commands that power everything else.

Mark 12:28–34 records one of the most compelling conversations in Scripture. A scribe (someone trained in the law) had been watching Jesus shut down shallow arguments from the religious elite. But this man wasn't trying to trap Jesus. He had a sincere question. *"Which commandment is the most important of all?"*

Instead of choosing from the Ten Commandments or quoting something trendy from the prophets, Jesus reached to the core of what God has always wanted from His people. *"Love God with all your heart, with all your soul, with all your mind, and with all your strength" (Mark 12:30).* Then, as if to say, "You can't separate this," He added, *"Love your neighbor as yourself" (Mark 12:31).*

Jesus didn't offer a list; He offered a lens. Everything else flows from these two commands. They aren't just priorities; they're the framework.

Notice how brilliantly simple yet impossibly comprehensive this is. Love for God covers the vertical relationship—your worship, devotion, and surrender. Love for neighbor covers the horizontal relationship—your interactions, service, and sacrifice. These two commands create a cross pattern that intersects at the heart of human existence. Every ethical dilemma, every relational conflict, every major life decision can be filtered through this dual command. It's like having GPS coordinates for the soul. No matter where you are or what you're facing, these commands can redirect you home.

What's compelling is that the scribe immediately agreed. He even added that love for God and neighbor matters more than all the religious rituals combined. Jesus affirmed him and said, *"You are not far from the kingdom of God"* *(Mark 12:34).*

But pause on that: *not far.* He wasn't in the kingdom yet…just close. Because understanding truth is not the same as embodying it. The hardest part is moving from insight to obedience. The kingdom isn't inherited by those who nod in agreement. It belongs to those who respond.

CALL TO ACTION #1: Audit your love distribution. Loving God with "all" means every category of your life. Heart. Soul. Mind. Strength. Are you giving God full access to your desires, thoughts, and choices? Or are there areas you've kept separate—your finances, your schedule, your attitude toward others?

CALL TO ACTION #2: Close the gap between knowing and doing. Don't be content with being close. Take a step. Pick one specific way today to show love to God more intentionally and one clear action to love someone else, even if it costs you.

The commands aren't just inspirational; they're foundational. They're not meant to be admired from a distance but lived up close. Love God fully. Love people authentically. That's the code that makes everything else make sense.

59. Jesus, The Mind-Bender
~Mark 12:35-37~

"How can the scribes say that the Messiah is the son of David? David himself says by the Holy Spirit: The Lord declared to my Lord, 'Sit at my right hand until I put your enemies under your feet.' David himself calls him 'Lord.' How, then, can he be his son?"
Mark 12:35-37 (CSB)

AFTER a full day of fielding hot takes from the religious elite, Jesus throws out a question that stops everyone in their tracks. This wasn't just a theological curveball; it was a direct hit to their assumptions about who the Messiah was supposed to be.

MARK 12:35-37 shows Jesus doing something unexpected: asking His own question instead of just answering theirs. The religious leaders had been grilling Him all day, but now He turns the tables with a mind-bender about David calling the Messiah "Lord" in Psalm 110.

The setup: everyone knew the Messiah would be David's descendant, his "son." But Jesus points out that David, writing under the Spirit's inspiration, calls this future descendant "my Lord." How can someone be both your son and your superior? It's like your great-great-grandson being your boss.

"The large crowd was listening to him with delight" (Mark 12:37), probably because Jesus was exposing the religious experts' incomplete understanding. But this wasn't just a clever riddle; Jesus was revealing His true identity. He's both David's son (fully human) and David's Lord (fully divine). The Messiah they were expecting was standing right in front of them, but He was so much more than their categories could contain.

The religious leaders went silent. Sometimes the most profound truth leaves you speechless.

CALL TO ACTION #1: Quit domesticating the divine. Stop trying to make Jesus fit your comfort zone and let Him blow your mind instead. Jesus refuses to be reduced to whatever role feels most convenient for you. He won't stay in the neat theological box you've built or limit Himself to the version of God that makes sense with your current lifestyle. When you find yourself thinking you've got Jesus figured out, that's probably when you need to sit in the mystery a little longer. Let Him be bigger than your theology, wilder than your expectations, and more surprising than your plans.

CALL TO ACTION #2: Let truth silence your debates. When Jesus speaks, stop arguing and start listening. The religious leaders went quiet because sometimes truth is so profound it leaves you speechless. Stop trying to win every theological argument and start letting God's Word transform you. Spend time in prayer without talking, just listening. Choose wonder over winning in your faith conversations. Some aspects of God are meant to be worshiped, not understood.

Jesus wasn't just answering a theological question; He was revealing Himself as the answer to humanity's deepest need. The same Jesus who confounded the experts with His wisdom wants to confound your limited expectations with His unlimited love.

60. Spiritual Veneers
~Mark 12:38-40~

"Beware of the scribes, who want to go around in long robes and who want greetings in the marketplaces, the best seats in the synagogues, and the places of honor at banquets. They devour widows' houses and say long prayers just for show. These will receive a harsher judgment."
Mark 12:38-40 (CSB)

THERE'S a big difference between being spiritual and looking spiritual. When filters frame everything and applause often outweighs authenticity, it's dangerously easy to care more about looking godly than actually being close to God.

Jesus confronted this in Mark 12:38-40. He wasn't talking to skeptics or pagans, He was calling out the respected religious leaders. These guys had the look: flowing robes that signaled status, public greetings that fed their egos, VIP seats in the synagogue, and all the attention they could ever want. On the outside they were spiritual icons. But underneath? It was all an act.

Jesus saw past the presentation. He pointed out the cracks in their foundation. While they were polishing their public image, they were taking advantage of widows (some of the most vulnerable people in society) and using long, dramatic prayers to cover it up. They weren't just hypocrites; they were predators in religious clothing.

That's why Jesus didn't just warn the crowd. He said these leaders would receive greater judgment. Because when you hold a position of spiritual influence, what you do with that influence matters more. And when you use the name of God to elevate yourself while oppressing others, the damage multiplies.

But here's the scary part: most people don't start fake. Somewhere along the way, applause becomes more addictive than obedience. Recognition feels better than repentance. They trade real intimacy with God for curated impressions of holiness. They learn to speak fluent religion while quietly drifting from the heart of God.

This passage isn't just a warning for leaders; it's a mirror for all of us. Have you gotten good at pretending? Have you become more concerned with looking faithful than actually living faithful? Do people see a version of you that isn't completely real?

Jesus isn't looking for perfect presentation. He's after spiritual honesty. He doesn't want fake smiles or memorized prayers. He wants your heart—even the messy, unfiltered parts.

CALL TO ACTION #1: Let God deal with the root, not just the surface. Get honest. Ask Him to expose what's behind the image.

CALL TO ACTION #2: Focus on real growth, not just spiritual optics. Invest in the quiet, unseen disciplines that build lasting character. True spiritual authority doesn't come from appearances or applause. It comes from a real connection with God—a life formed in secret, not just performed in public.

61. Granny Can Ball
~Mark 12:41-44~

Sitting across from the temple treasury, he watched how the crowd dropped money into the treasury. Many rich people were putting in large sums. Then a poor widow came and dropped in two tiny coins worth very little. Mark 12:41-42 (CSB)

WHILE everyone else was shooting three-pointers with their big donations, one woman came off the bench and dunked so hard she broke the entire scoring system.

Mark gives us one of the most beautiful game-changers in Scripture. Jesus is courtside at the temple treasury, watching the offering game unfold. The rich players are putting up impressive numbers, throwing in *large sums*—probably making quite the show of their financial athleticism.

Then comes a poor widow with two small copper coins, worth about a penny total. She quietly steps up to the line and drops in what looks like the weakest shot of the day. But Jesus sees something everyone else missed. He calls His disciples over because this woman just shattered the backboard.

He announces, *"This poor widow has put more into the treasury than all the others"* (Mark 12:43). The disciples are probably thinking, "Coach, check the scoreboard." But Jesus explains the new math: *"They all gave out of their surplus, but she out of her poverty has put in everything she had—all she had to live on"* (Mark 12:44).

The rich were playing with house money. She bet everything she had. They gave from their bench strength. She gave her starting lineup. In God's arena, the percentage of sacrifice matters more than the dollar amount on the scoreboard. Her two-cent donation was a full-court miracle shot that changed the entire game.

CALL TO ACTION #1: Play by heaven's scoring system. Stop measuring your generosity by the amount and start measuring it by the sacrifice. God doesn't keep score the way the world does. Your $20 gift might outrank someone else's $2,000 if it represents a bigger sacrifice. Calculate the real cost of your giving by asking whether your gifts actually require you to trust God or just clean out your spare change. Give until it matters, until you have to adjust other spending and rely on God's provision. Focus on faithfulness over flashiness.

CALL TO ACTION #2: Scout for the overlooked MVPs. Start recognizing the people God celebrates even when the world ignores them. The widow's performance was invisible to everyone except Jesus. Who are the overlooked MVPs in your world? The single mom working two jobs, the elderly neighbor who prays for everyone, the volunteer who shows up every week without recognition. Notice them. Encourage them. Celebrate their faithfulness. Invest in ministries and causes that may not be glamorous but are making real impact.

The widow's two coins teach us that God doesn't need our money; He wants our hearts. When we give sacrificially, we're not funding God's work; we're joining His team.

Her gift looked small by human standards but was legendary by heaven's standards. In God's arena, it's not about how much you have; it's about how much you're willing to put on the line.

62. When Your Aesthetic Expires
~Mark 13:1-2~

Jesus said to him, "Do you see these great buildings? Not one stone will be left upon another—all will be thrown down."
Mark 13:2 (CSB)

TOUR a perfectly curated life with designer wardrobe, tastefully modern house, and envy-worthy Instagram feed, and it's easy to believe it's solid, permanent, untouchable.

The disciples had that same reaction when they marveled at the temple in Jerusalem. Its massive stones, shining gold, and national significance made it the apex of spiritual success and cultural power. But Jesus wasn't impressed. He told them: *"Not one stone will be left upon another—all will be thrown down."* That had to be jarring. This wasn't just architecture; it was identity. The temple represented centuries of faith, history and national pride.

But Jesus saw something the disciples didn't: beneath all the religious beauty, the foundation was cracking. The temple had become a monument to human power, not a house of prayer. The warning wasn't about the building; it was about misplacing trust. Jesus knew that anything we worship other than God will eventually collapse.

And in 70 A.D., this became reality. The temple was torn apart by Roman forces, just as Jesus said. God had allowed sacred spaces to fall before. Solomon's original temple was destroyed by Babylon centuries earlier. Even the most holy places on earth aren't immune to judgement when they stop serving their purpose.

The lesson shows that tradition without genuine devotion becomes empty ritual. Beautiful buildings without transformed hearts become monuments to pride rather than worship. We still chase temples. They're careers, platforms, homes, or reputations, but if they're rooted in status or appearance, they won't hold up when pressure comes.

The truth? Most of what we obsess over won't make it into the next generation, much less eternity. Consider how quickly yesterday's "must-have" becomes today's outdated trend. The phone you couldn't live without three years ago now feels ancient. The career achievement that once defined your worth gets overshadowed by accomplishments. The relationship status that seemed so important shifts with time. Even our most prized possessions and achievements have expiration dates stamped on them from the beginning.

Jesus wasn't trying to shame the disciples. He was trying to shift their vision. He wanted them and us to recognize what lasts. It's not your curated feed. It's not your career wins. It's your soul, your relationships, your obedience to God when no one else sees. The things of this world will fade. That's not cause for despair…it's freedom. When we stop building lives around what won't last, we're finally free to invest in what will.

CALL TO ACTION #1: Stop chasing temporary validation. Refocus on becoming someone of character, not just someone who looks successful.

CALL TO ACTION #2: Prioritize what outlasts you. Give your best energy to spiritual growth, real friendships, and kingdom impact. Let your imminent expiration date push you to live for something more. Jesus wasn't impressed with temples, and He's not impressed with facades. He's looking for hearts fully surrendered because those are the lives that stand when everything else falls.

63. Don't Fall For The Hype
~Mark 13:3-8~

"Watch out that no one deceives you." Mark 13:5-6 (CSB)

EVERYWHERE you look, someone is selling a secret formula. Fast-track success, instant peace, effortless relationships. It's all packaged with bold claims and flashy confidence. But Jesus warned that in times of uncertainty, false voices would rise offering hope that sounds convincing but leads nowhere.

When the disciples asked Him about the end of the age, they expected signs and timelines. Instead, Jesus started with a warning: *"Watch out that no one deceives you."* That might not sound dramatic, but it is absolutely essential. He knew that chaos creates vulnerability. When life feels unstable, people grab onto anything that offers a sense of control or clarity.

Jesus didn't say there would be peace and calm. He spoke of wars, earthquakes, famines, and global upheaval. But then He said something surprising: *"These are the beginning of birth pains" (Mark 13:8).* He compared the distress of this world not to collapse, but to labor. Meaning, something new is on the way.

Birth pains are intense and unpredictable, but they do not signal the end. They are signs of new life coming. In the same way, Jesus was telling His followers not to be overwhelmed by fear when the world feels like it is unraveling. These struggles point toward God's plan unfolding, not falling apart.

And yet, during these moments, people often look for a shortcut. That is when false messiahs and self-proclaimed saviors show up. Some claim to have special insight. Others twist Scripture to fit their message. But Jesus said clearly in Mark 13:6 that many would be deceived.

Deception is rarely obvious. It mimics truth just enough to feel right. That is why Jesus taught His disciples to be alert. Not just awake to events around them, but awake to what Scripture actually teaches.

We still live in a world that trades truth for hype. That turns fear into clicks and confusion into profit. But Jesus never called us to chase predictions or follow personalities. He called us to stay grounded in Him.

CALL TO ACTION #1: Pay attention to what you're believing. Compare it to God's Word. Filter out the noise and seek wisdom from Scripture and trusted mentors.

CALL TO ACTION #2: Stay steady when the world shakes. Turn your focus to prayer, gratitude, and daily rhythms that keep your heart anchored in God's peace. Staying alert is not about being anxious. It is about knowing who you trust and why.

1

1

RYAN HELLER

64. Stand Your Ground
~Mark 13:9-13~

"You will be hated by everyone because of my name, but the one who endures to the end will be saved." Mark 13:13 (CSB)

PUBLIC shaming campaigns are real and standing up for your beliefs can cost you friendships, job opportunities, or social standing. Jesus didn't sugarcoat this reality for His followers. He promised they'd be dragged through courts, turned away by family members, and hated by people in general because of their faith. But He also promised something powerful: the Holy Spirit would give them words to speak when they needed them most.

Notice Jesus didn't say "if" you face opposition but "when." Following Christ authentically will create friction with a world that operates on different values. This isn't because Christians are supposed to be obnoxious or judgmental, but because the gospel itself challenges the fundamental assumptions of human pride and self-sufficiency.

Jesus described specific types of persecution His followers would face. They'd be dragged before religious and political authorities, betrayed by family members, and hated by society in general. This wasn't theoretical; it was prophetic. The early church experienced exactly what Jesus predicted, and Christians around the world continue to face these realities today.

But persecution isn't punishment; it's purpose. Your faithfulness during hard times becomes a testimony that can change hearts. When people see you respond to mistreatment with love, maintain joy during suffering, and continue serving others despite personal cost, they witness

150

something supernatural. The Holy Spirit uses these moments to reveal God's character through your character.

Jesus promised that when believers are brought before authorities, they shouldn't worry about what to say because the Holy Spirit will give them the right words. This doesn't mean we shouldn't prepare or study, but it means we can trust God to help us communicate His truth effectively when we're under pressure.

The phrase *the one who endures to the end will be saved* doesn't mean we earn salvation through endurance. Rather, it means that genuine faith perseveres through trials. Those who truly belong to Christ will continue following Him even when it's costly, because the Holy Spirit gives them strength to endure.

Standing firm doesn't mean being stubborn or refusing to listen to others. It means maintaining your commitment to Christ and His truth even when the pressure is intense. It means choosing obedience to God over approval from people, and eternal values over temporary comfort.

CALL TO ACTION #1: Prepare mentally and spiritually for the cost of following Jesus publicly. Build your faith muscles now so you'll be strong when opposition comes. Practice sharing your faith story in low-pressure situations first. Build relationships with other believers who can encourage you during tough times. Study how biblical characters handled persecution to learn from their examples.

CALL TO ACTION #2: Trust the Holy Spirit to guide your words when you face opposition. Depend on God's wisdom rather than your own cleverness when defending your faith. Pray for wisdom before entering difficult conversations about faith. Memorize key Bible verses that explain the gospel clearly. Focus on speaking truth with love rather than winning arguments.

65. No Time To Pack Your Bags
~Mark 13:14-23~

"When you see the abomination of desolation standing where it should not be" (let the reader understand), "then those in Judea must flee to the mountains." Mark 13:14 (CSB)

IF your smoke alarm went off in the middle of the night and you smelled smoke, you wouldn't scroll through your notifications or grab your favorite sneakers. You'd bounce. Fast. That kind of instant reaction is exactly what Jesus was describing in Mark 13.

He was talking about a time of intense crisis, a specific moment when destruction would hit Jerusalem. When His followers saw the sign He warned about, they weren't supposed to stick around and figure things out. They were supposed to drop everything and go.

Jesus' warning isn't just about a history lesson; it has real-time relevance for your life right now. He's teaching a deeper truth that there are moments in life when your obedience to God needs to be immediate. No hesitations. No what-ifs. No trying to pack your bags with the stuff you think you'll need to be comfortable along the way.

And here's the challenge for a lot of us. We're carrying stuff we're way too attached to. Maybe it's a relationship we know God is nudging us to surrender. Maybe it's our image, success, or that unhealthy habit that makes us feel in control. Jesus is saying when it's time to follow Him, you need to be free enough to move without delay.

This isn't about being reckless or impulsive. It's about being prepared spiritually. The early Christians who heeded Jesus' warning and fled Jerusalem before the Roman siege in 70 A.D. survived because they had cultivated the discipline of immediate obedience. They had already learned to prioritize God's voice over their own comfort or convenience. Their spiritual reflexes were sharp because they had been practicing surrender in smaller ways all along.

Jesus understood the mindset of people back then, and He totally understands ours today. He knew there would be plenty of distractions, fake voices, spiritual noise, and cultural chaos trying to pull us away from what's real. That is why He warned us to stay sharp. The only way to stay grounded is to be so familiar with His voice that everything else fades into the background. That kind of clarity comes from walking with Him consistently, choosing obedience one step at a time.

The difference between spiritual preparation and spiritual panic is daily practice. When crisis comes, those who have been regularly listening, surrendering, and obeying will respond with faith. Those who have been putting off obedience will hesitate when swift action is required.

CALL TO ACTION #1: Develop a "go now" mindset when it comes to obeying God. Stop putting off what you know He's asking you to do. Whether it's reaching out in kindness, letting go of a toxic pattern, or finally taking that leap of faith, do it today. Practice fast faith: hear, trust, obey.

CALL TO ACTION #2: Don't let attachment to temporary things prevent you from following God's direction. Hold loosely to possessions and comforts that might hinder your obedience. Regularly evaluate what possessions or comforts might be holding you back spiritually. Practice generosity by giving away things you're too attached to. Choose obedience to God over comfort or convenience when they conflict.

66. The Hero's Return
~Mark 13:24-27~

Then they will see the Son of Man coming in clouds with great power and glory. Mark 13:26 (CSB)

THERE'S a reason we're drawn to stories about epic comebacks. Whether it's in comics, films, or books, we love watching the hero return when everything seems lost, stepping in with power to turn it all around. That's not just fiction. There's a reason it resonates so deeply in our hearts. It taps into something our souls already know is real. Jesus spoke of a day when He, the true King, will return in undeniable and unstoppable power.

After warning His disciples about the chaos and suffering that would come, Jesus quickly turned to the future: His return. Jesus painted a picture of cosmic upheaval, the sun going dark, the moon losing its glow, stars crashing from the heavens as if the universe itself was hitting the pause button to make room for its Creator. And then, He arrives...not the humble Teacher from Galilee, but the glorious King coming in the clouds. No one will miss it.

Son of Man isn't just a catchy title. It's a direct callback to Daniel 7, where the phrase refers to someone who's given authority, glory and an unstoppable kingdom. Jesus is saying that's Him. Back in Daniel 7, the ancient prophecy said, *"A kingdom that will never be destroyed."* Jesus is saying, "That's me."

It's not just that He's coming back. He's coming back to bring it to a conclusion. In Mark 13:27, Jesus says He will send out angels to gather His people from everywhere, from all around, from all over, from every direction and every location. No believer is getting left behind. Front row seats

154

or nosebleed section, if you're a part of Jesus, you're getting called in. It's a cosmic, global reunion.

All the injustice, the pain, the evil in this world will not have the last word. Christ's return guarantees that. He's not showing up to be a part of the action. He's showing up to end it. In a flash. Completely.

If you're a follower of Jesus, this is the future we can hang on to as everything around us seems to be falling apart. This world, with all its struggles and pain, is not the end. We belong to a kingdom that's still on the way. But if you're not a follower of Jesus yet, this is not just a cool future event. This is a warning. There's no time like the present. The future is coming. Time is running out. What we believe about the future should impact how we live today.

CALL TO ACTION #1: Live with confident hope knowing Jesus will return and make all things right.
Let the promise of His return sustain you through present difficulties and injustices. Write down current struggles and pray about how God's justice will prevail. Encourage others who are suffering by reminding them of Christ's promised return. Make decisions based on eternal perspective rather than temporary circumstances.

CALL TO ACTION #2: Stay ready for Christ's return by living faithfully today. Use the time you have left to advance His kingdom and prepare for eternity. Examine your life for areas that need repentance and make those changes now. Share the gospel with people who don't know Jesus yet. Use your gifts and resources to advance God's kingdom while there's still time.

67. Rerouting Not Required
~Mark 13:28-31~

"Heaven and earth will pass away, but my words will never pass away." Mark 13:31 (CSB)

HAVE you ever been driving in a new area when your GPS suddenly announced, "Rerouting"? The panic that ensues is real! Did you miss a turn? Did you disregard a direction? It is unsettling when you feel shaky about where you are going.

The promise of Mark 13:31 steadies our hearts: *"Heaven and earth will pass away, but my words will never pass away."* Unlike the places and seasons we navigate through, God's word is reliable and solid. Jesus says, "I'm the one who remains the same. When everything else is shifting, changing, vanishing, trust what I say. For my words will never fade or alter." He offers clarity when our current GPS and voices lack transparency.

Our world is used to endless notifications, platforms that rewrite what we read, and opinions that are swayed hourly. But God's word does not react. It is steadfast. It is eternal. It does not shift with time or trend. It will always lead with truth.

GPS apps reroute us to dead ends or unfamiliar highways. Headlines and influencers point us in contradicting directions. Internal thoughts can reroute us to fear, regret, anxiety or pressure. But Scripture always points in the right direction. It doesn't guess. It knows. It doesn't need updates.

Imagine the disciples who heard Jesus say these words. They were navigating shifting political seasons, religious disagreements, and social conflict. Their entire worldview was being transformed.

Jesus anchored them in an eternal foundation. He chose to root them in His word and His truth. It gave them confidence, not because of their circumstances but because of who He was.

Choosing to follow God's Word is not about weighing pros and cons. It is a decision to start from a place that does not fail. Jesus is not our backup; He is our roadmap. When we begin with God's word, we do not need to recalculate; we simply need to follow.

The amazing thing about God's word is that it speaks into every season, every struggle, every victory. Scripture offers guidance that goes far beyond your current situation. It doesn't just give you answers; it shapes you into the image of Christ.

CALL TO ACTION #1: Write down one decision where you have been navigating by outside advice, emotion, or instinct, rather than bringing it before God. Ask Him to illuminate it with His word. Pray for one verse connected to that situation. Let His word be your anchor.

CALL TO ACTION #2: Speak Scripture over your routine. Pick one verse each day that speaks to God's character or His promises. Say it multiple times throughout your day. Let it influence your focus, thoughts, interactions, and voice.

When the fear of the unknown or uncertainty reroutes you, remember that God's word is not swayed by time, culture, or technology. It is trustworthy, timeless, and true. Let His direction chart your course. Forget the reroutes. Follow the One who always leads with absolute accuracy.

68. Stay Awake, Stay Ready
~Mark 13:32-37~

"Therefore be alert, since you don't know when the master of the house is coming—whether in the evening or at midnight or at the crowing of the rooster or early in the morning." Mark 13:35 (CSB)

NOBODY knows when that phone will ring and life will never be the same—the offer of a new job, the urgent situation that needs immediate attention, the moment when someone needs you and only you can help. Wise people remain prepared and ready to respond. Jesus taught a similar lesson about His coming. Because no one knows the day or hour, everyone should remain spiritually watchful and ready. He likened it to servants awaiting their master's return from a journey.

Jesus made it crystal clear that even He didn't know the exact timing of His return while He was on earth. Only the Father knows that information. This should humble anyone who claims to have figured out the date or thinks they can predict when the end will come. If Jesus didn't know the timing during His earthly ministry, we certainly shouldn't pretend we do.

The parable Jesus told is straightforward. A man goes on a journey and leaves his servants in charge of his house. Each servant has specific responsibilities, and the doorkeeper is told to stay alert because the master could return at any time. The point isn't to live in constant anxiety but to maintain faithful readiness.

The key word is: *"Watch!" (Mark 13:33).* This isn't passive waiting but active readiness. Like a security guard on duty or an athlete in training, followers of Jesus maintain spiritual alertness. We live fully in the present while staying prepared for eternity. This means taking care of our responsibilities, serving others, and growing in our relationship with God.

Jesus emphasized this point by repeating it: *"Be alert!"* *(Mark 13:33)*. He knew that people would be tempted to either panic about His return or become complacent and forget about it entirely. Both extremes miss the mark. We're called to live with confident expectation, not fearful anxiety or careless indifference.

The uncertainty of timing is actually a gift. It keeps us dependent on God rather than trying to control the future. It motivates us to live faithfully every day rather than procrastinating until we think the end is near. It helps us focus on our character and relationships rather than getting obsessed with prophetic speculation.

Living ready doesn't mean selling everything and sitting on a mountain waiting for Jesus. It means being the kind of person who could meet Jesus today without shame or regret. It means loving God and others well, using our gifts faithfully, and staying spiritually alert to what God is doing around us.

CALL TO ACTION #1: Maintain spiritual alertness through consistent daily practices. Build habits that keep you connected to God and aware of His activity. Establish a morning routine that includes prayer and Bible reading. Set phone reminders throughout the day to pause and pray briefly.

CALL TO ACTION #2: Live each day as if Jesus could return today while planning responsibly for the future. Balance eternal perspective with faithful stewardship of your current responsibilities. Make peace with people you've had conflicts with instead of putting it off. Use your talents and resources generously rather than hoarding them. Share your faith boldly since you don't know how much time remains.

69. Image Over Integrity
~Mark 14:1-2~

The chief priests and the scribes were looking for a cunning way to arrest Jesus and kill him. Mark 14:1 (CSB)

IT was a busy week in Jerusalem. The city was full of visitors and celebrations, and everyone was in their finest attire. It was a holiday week with festival electricity. Imagine Woodstock meets a church camp reunion. The town was bustling with activity and visible joy from the throngs of attendees. But not all of Jerusalem was on display for the public to see.

Behind closed doors and out of sight of the masses, things were very different. The spiritual leaders were hatching a plan. A plot to target not a political foe or foreign invader, but Jesus Himself. These were not some lowly renegades. No. These were the bigwigs. The people with lengthy titles, résumés, and approval ratings. So why the covertness? Because optics were everything. They were far more concerned about what the crowd might think than they were about doing what would please God. It wasn't just fear of a negative response that had them operating in the shadows. But also fear of losing control, power, and position.

Sound familiar? Image is the currency of our modern time. Platforms are polished and curated. Feedback is filtered. Cancel culture is indeed a threat at every turn. The temptation to appear pious while protecting our pettiness is as real today as it was in Jerusalem 2000 years ago. Influence can be valued over integrity. Faith can be practiced as performance art instead of lived from the inside out.

These religious big shots were well versed in putting on a good face while harboring murder in their hearts. They could recite the right prayers, wear the right clothes, and sit in the seats of honor. But their hearts were far from God. They had worked so hard to get to where they were in their religious circles that they would not allow the Messiah to come and dismantle their kingdom.

We can pull up in the right neighborhood, repost something from church, and memorize a verse without ever letting it penetrate our hearts. We can look religious without being required to be radical. But Jesus never asked us to be filtered followers. He called us to full surrender, which sometimes costs us comfort and control and crowd approval. Jesus knows the face you put on for others. He knows the front you display for friends. But He also knows the reality of what lives in your heart.

CALL TO ACTION #1: Invite the Holy Spirit to show you where your spiritual presence trumps your obedience in private. Journal one area where you are operating for reputation rather than repentance. Commit today to being honest before God about your heart.

CALL TO ACTION #2: Shift your focus from audience to authenticity. In any space where you influence others (online, at work, or in your friend group), let your private devotion match your public expression. Speak from genuine faith, not filtered performance. Let your life preach louder than your posts.

70. The Performance Review
~Mark 14:3-10~

Some were expressing indignation to one another: "Why has this perfume been wasted? For this perfume might have been sold for more than three hundred denarii and given to the poor." And they began to scold her. Mark 14:4-5 (CSB)

SOMEONE interrupted a worship night by pulling out a year's salary and spending it in one single moment of devotion. No livestream. No audience. Just pure affection for Jesus. That's how it was when a woman poured out her expensive perfume to anoint Him.

The response? Instant backlash. The people in the room didn't whisper their disapproval. They scolded her out loud. Their critique came dressed up as wisdom. It sounded like a budget proposal with a moral backbone. "This could've been used to help the poor." But Jesus wasn't buying it, and neither should we.

Mark tells us the perfume was worth about 300 denarii. That's not a minor gift. This was an intentional, extravagant act of worship. She wasn't trying to be practical. She was showing that Jesus was worth it all. What looked like waste to them was worship to Him.

The critics didn't see her heart; they saw her value through the lens of efficiency. Jesus saw the opposite. He said, *"She has done a noble thing for me"* (Mark 14:6). While everyone else calculated the cost, she gave without hesitation.

And there's a deeper twist: Judas, the one who led the charge in criticizing her, was stealing from the ministry funds. His objection wasn't about compassion; it was about control. He wanted the money in the bag he was robbing from.

The whole scene reads like a performance review where the one doing the grading is actually the most off track. It's easy to mask greed with concern. It's easy to cover control with spiritual language. But Jesus sees through the layers.

This story forces us to ask, do we value what others bring to Jesus? Or do we critique what doesn't make sense to us? Are we pouring ourselves out for Him or calculating what it might cost our reputation? Worship is not always neat, efficient, or explainable. But it is noticed.

Jesus said, *"Wherever the gospel is proclaimed... what she has done will be told in memory of her" (Mark 14:9).*

CALL TO ACTION #1: Before you critique someone's worship, ask yourself what's really driving your reaction. Is it jealousy? Insecurity? Pride? Let the Holy Spirit expose what's underneath before you speak over someone else's offering.

CALL TO ACTION #2: Live with open hands. Let generosity flow from devotion, not performance. Ask God to make your heart more sensitive to His presence than to public opinion and give from that place of love.

71. Cancel Your Plans
~Mark 14:12-16~

So he sent two of his disciples and told them, "Go into the city, and a man carrying a jar of water will meet you. Follow him."
Mark 14:13 (CSB)

WE spend our days making backup plans for our backup plans. We check the weather twice, save multiple drafts, and keep spare chargers in every bag. The illusion of control feels safer than surrender, even when our planning falls apart anyway. But what if overplanning reveals our lack of faith? In His final week prior to the crucifixion, Jesus shows us a different way—one that should make us question whether or not our white-knuckle grip on details is actually helping us.

When the disciples need to prepare for Passover, Jesus doesn't brainstorm options or create contingency plans. He doesn't say, "Let's scout locations," or "Call me if something goes wrong." Instead, He gives them instructions so specific and confident that they sound almost absurd. He tells them exactly who they'll meet, where they'll go, and what they'll find as if He's already lived this moment.

A jar of water? In that culture, men didn't usually carry water jars. This was like telling a friend today to meet a businessman riding a scooter through Target. It would have been an immediately obvious identifier.

What's even more remarkable is what happens next. The disciples don't end up with a general area or best guess. They find the exact man, house, and room that Jesus said they would. He said it would be ready and so it was. It was already prepared before they showed up. No last-minute dash. God already had it arranged.

What we see in this moment is proof that even as the plot to kill Jesus thickened, even as His closest friends began to fight, He was still in control. Nothing was happening without His direction. Nothing He said was reactionary. Everything from that moment until the cross was planned in advance.

Jesus was not blindsided. He was leading the story of His passion, even as the plot grew around Him If you need evidence that God is still in control right now, the perfect dinner is a good place to start.

When our dates cancel, our jobs fold, or our prayers feel delayed, we can get it in our heads that God is quiet or absent. The reality is that pieces may already be moving behind the scenes. God never needs to drop the sky to prove He is in control. Sometimes it's most evident in under-appreciated details.

The disciples likely expected to spend the evening negotiating, planning, and strategizing. What they got instead was rest. The ease that comes with obeying. The realization that their part is to simply listen and follow, not make everything happen. They were not in charge. Jesus was. And the further we lean into what God is telling us, the more we realize truth.

CALL TO ACTION #1: Surrender your timeline. Stop trying to force events to go your way. Give God time to work. Let obedience silence the voice that wants control.

CALL TO ACTION #2: Remember where you've seen God come through. Write down answered prayers, miraculous moments of provision, and times when God showed up. Let these notes remind you of days He has made.

72. The Betrayal Bomb
~Mark 14:17-21~

"Truly I tell you, one of you will betray me—one who is eating with me." Mark 14:18 (CSB)

THE most painful betrayals do not come from enemies. They come from people who know your Netflix password. People who have shared meals, inside jokes, and late-night conversations. That is what makes betrayal so personal; it wears the face of someone you once trusted.

In Mark 14:17–21, Jesus drops a shocking statement during dinner: *"One of you will betray me."* Not a religious leader from the outside. Not a Roman soldier. One of them. One of the Twelve. One of the guys who had walked miles with Him, prayed beside Him, and watched miracles unfold.

The room went silent. The disciples, stunned, each asked, *"Surely not I?" (Mark 14:19).* It is the question we all ask when we hear about someone falling away. But what makes this moment more disturbing is that Judas, already set on betraying Jesus, stayed at the table. He kept pretending. Kept passing the bread. Kept looking like part of the team while his heart had already walked out the door.

Jesus knew exactly what Judas had done. Still, He let him sit at the table. He washed his feet. He served him food. He gave him opportunity after opportunity to turn back. Jesus showed love in the face of betrayal, and that should stop us in our tracks.

This story is not just about Judas. It is also about us. We are quick to distance ourselves from the traitor, but sometimes we are not that different. We keep showing up in the right places while hiding a heart that is drifting. We

166

say the right words but ignore the quiet convictions that ask us to change.

Spiritual drift never looks dramatic at first. It's subtle. Slow. Silent. We nod our heads in worship while quietly numbing our conviction. We keep one foot in God's presence and the other in our private plan. Judas wasn't the only one pretending at the table. We all wear masks sometimes. But the grace of Jesus invites us to remove them.

Jesus never stopped loving Judas, and He never stops loving us. But He does call us to examine what is really happening beneath the surface. Betrayal rarely starts big. It begins with small compromises. Self-interest. Secret plans. And eventually, it leads us away from the One who never stopped including us.

CALL TO ACTION #1: Forgive the person who hurt you. Release the offense, pray for them by name, and ask God to heal the wound instead of rehearsing it.

CALL TO ACTION #2: Confront your own duplicity. Bring your hidden motives into the light. Repent, realign with God's truth, and invite someone to help you stay accountable.

73. Blood Bank Of Heaven
~Mark 14:22-26~

He said to them, "This is my blood of the covenant, which is poured out for many." Mark 14:24 (CSB)

BLOOD banks save lives every day through voluntary donations, but Mark 14:22-26 describes the ultimate blood donation—one that saves souls for eternity. When Jesus lifted the cup and said, *"This is my blood of the covenant, which is poured out for many,"* He wasn't speaking metaphorically. He was announcing the greatest exchange in human history.

The Maximum Contract

IN ancient covenants, blood sealed the deal. It represented life itself being poured out to guarantee the promise. When Jesus declared His blood would be poured out for many, He was signing a contract with His own life. The terms? His perfect life in exchange for our broken ones. His innocence for our guilt. His death for our eternal life.

The disciples didn't fully grasp what they were witnessing. They thought they were sharing a traditional Passover meal, but Jesus was instituting something revolutionary. The bread represented His body, broken for them. The wine represented His blood, shed for the forgiveness of sins.

This wasn't just a symbolic gesture; it was a prophetic declaration. Within hours, Jesus would literally give His body and blood on the cross to purchase our salvation. The Last Supper was both a memorial of what was about to happen and a promise of what it would accomplish.

The Eternal Transfusion

JESUS offered a one-time transaction that became an eternal transfusion. His blood doesn't just cover our sin; it transforms our DNA from death to life, from condemnation to righteousness, from separation to intimate relationship with God.

When we take communion today, we're not just remembering a historical event but celebrating an ongoing reality. His blood still speaks. His covenant still stands. His life flows through us.

The power of Jesus' blood isn't just about forgiveness but about transformation. It doesn't just change our legal status before God; it changes our actual nature. We become new creations, with new hearts and new power to live differently.

The Covenant That Never Expires

UNLIKE human contracts that have expiration dates and escape clauses, Jesus' blood covenant is eternal and unconditional. It's not based on our performance or faithfulness; it's based on His character and sacrifice.

When we fail, the blood still covers us. When we doubt, the covenant still holds. When we feel unworthy, His worthiness becomes ours. This is the security that comes from being blood-bought children of God.

The communion table reminds us that we belong to Jesus, not because we earned it, but because He purchased us. We're not trying to maintain our salvation through good works; we're celebrating the salvation He already accomplished through His sacrifice.

The Invitation to Remember

"DO this in remembrance of me," Jesus said *(Luke 22:19)*. This wasn't just about mental recall; it was about active participation in the reality of His sacrifice. When we take communion, we're declaring our dependence on His blood for our salvation and our ongoing relationship with God.

This remembrance also connects us to believers throughout history and around the world. The same cup Jesus shared with His disciples is the cup we share today. The same covenant that saved the apostles is the covenant that saves us.

CALL TO ACTION #1: Live daily in the reality of what Christ's blood accomplished for you. Start each morning remembering that you are completely forgiven and accepted. Make decisions based on your new identity rather than past failures. Walk in the confidence that comes from being blood-bought and Spirit-filled. Let the security of His covenant give you courage to take risks for His kingdom.

CALL TO ACTION #2: Share the power of Christ's blood with others who need hope. Tell someone this week about the life change you've experienced through Jesus. Invite a friend to church or a Bible study to hear the gospel. Remember that the same blood that saved you can save anyone who believes.

The blood of Jesus is the most precious substance in the universe because it purchased the most valuable treasure—your soul. The covenant He signed with His life is the guarantee of your eternal security and the foundation of your daily confidence.

74. Courage Has A Curfew
~Mark 14:27-31~

But he kept insisting, "If I have to die with you, I will never deny you."
And they all said the same thing. Mark 14:31 (CSB)

FEAR has a way of getting the best of us. It's one thing to promise faithfulness in the daylight, surrounded by friends. It's another thing entirely when darkness sets in and staying silent feels safer than speaking up. We like to believe we're brave. We tell ourselves we'd never back down. But when the stakes rise, even the boldest voices can go quiet. Just ask Peter.

This situation in Mark's Gospel reads like a conversation full of conviction. Jesus says all of them will fall away. Peter argues. Hard. "Not me," he claims. He's so sure of his courage that he speaks over the warning. Everyone else chimes in too, echoing Peter's bold claim.

This scene feels familiar. Haven't we all made similar declarations? Haven't we sworn we'd never compromise our values, never stay silent when it matters, never choose comfort over conviction? In that upper room, surrounded by people who shared their beliefs, their promises felt unshakeable.

But Jesus isn't guessing. He knows exactly what's coming. The pressure, the confusion, the fear—it's all headed their way. And when it hits, the same men who stood tall in the upper room will scatter in the dark.

Peter's denial doesn't come from hate. It comes from fear. From exhaustion. From the chaos of watching everything fall apart faster than he expected. Courage, it turns out, has a curfew when it's built on emotion instead of understanding. When adrenaline fades and reality sets in,

171

good intentions aren't always enough to sustain bold actions.

This isn't just Peter's story. It's ours too. Every time we shrink back from what we believe to avoid discomfort, we echo this scene. Every time we keep quiet to fit in, we rehearse Peter's words. "I don't know Him." Not always with our mouths, but often with our silence.

Consider how many times we've promised God we'd be different, that we'd stand firm next time, that we'd speak up when it mattered. Yet when the pressure builds, when relationships are on the line, when our reputation might suffer, we find ourselves choosing safety over surrender.

The disciples weren't evil or faithless. They were human. They loved Jesus deeply, but their understanding was incomplete. They thought courage was about willpower and determination, not realizing it required divine strength and deeper preparation.

Jesus knew. And still, He kept Peter close. This is what makes the story powerful. Not that Peter failed, but that Jesus anticipated the failure and stayed anyway. He knew courage would collapse that night. But He also knew restoration was coming later.

Grace doesn't wait for perfect performance. It meets us in our failures and writes better endings than our mistakes would suggest. Peter's story doesn't end with denial; it ends with redemption, leadership, and a courage that finally matched his convictions.

CALL TO ACTION #1: Commit to one bold step this week. It could be a conversation, a post, a prayer out loud. Choose one space where fear has lingered and show up anyway.

CALL TO ACTION #2: Reflect on your "midnight moments." Think about a time you've denied your values or faith. What would grace say to you in that situation now?

75. Surrender Your Will
~Mark 14:32-42~

He said, "Abba, Father! All things are possible for you. Take this cup away from me. Nevertheless, not what I will, but what you will."
Mark 14:36 (CSB)

MANY of us live with fists clenched around plans, timelines, and our version of how life should go. We pray for God's will, but hope with all our hearts that it lines up with our own. Mark 14 reveals the God of the universe coming to earth and showing us what it looks like to open our hands and surrender everything we think we want for everything God knows we need.

Jesus wrestles in the garden. He sweats drops of blood. He cries out to His Father, asking if there is any other way. And then we get to that hinge of history: *"Nevertheless, not what I will, but what you will."* It's an act of surrender that is honest about the cost while choosing faithfulness and trust over control.

"Take this cup away from me" shows us Jesus' humanity. He doesn't just nod and say, "Fine, I'll do your will, God." He feels the weight of what's about to happen. He desperately wants an alternate path to unfold before Him. In this moment, Jesus models true surrender for us. He is willing to set aside His own desires and trust in the Father's greater plan. True faith doesn't mean we don't want our own way. It means we no longer grip that desire so tightly in our hands that we're unwilling to let it go.

This is where so many of us become stuck in the grappling of our own wills. We would love to surrender to God's will, but we need to see the outcome first. We can trust in God's will so long as it lines up with what we're already holding onto. But that isn't surrender. Jesus is showing us a different path: the path of surrender before we see the resurrection. Trusting before the tomb is empty. Choosing the Father's will even as He is staring down the cross.

The life of faith requires this posture from us, not just once in a season of crisis, but day after day. It requires us to release our death grip on relationships, careers, timelines, and outcomes. It requires us to pray, "Not my will, but yours," over our marriages, our children, our dreams, and our fears. It requires us to trust that the God who sent His Son to the cross has our best interests at heart, even when His path for us runs straight through the valleys we would rather avoid.

Surrender doesn't mean we passively resign ourselves to our fate. It means we actively trust that God's will, even when it looks nothing like our own, is always good, always loving, and always leads us toward life.

CALL TO ACTION #1: What are you gripping too tightly? Ask God to show you where you are trying to control outcomes instead of surrendering to His will. Surrender these areas to Him in prayer today.

CALL TO ACTION #2: Practice daily surrender. Begin each morning by praying the words of Jesus: "Not my will, but yours." Make this your default response when life doesn't go the way you planned.

76. Jesus Didn't Flinch
~Mark 14:43-52~

"Have you come out with swords and clubs, as if I were a criminal, to capture me? Every day I was among you...and you didn't arrest me. But the Scriptures must be fulfilled." Mark 14:48-49(CSB)

HAVE you ever been the only calm person in a group chat meltdown? Everyone's spiraling, blaming, overreacting, and you're just sitting there, reading the thread, knowing that none of it is helping. That's Jesus in the garden

The garden was packed with drama. Judas arrived with a squad, leading an armed crowd. Peter panicked and sliced off a guy's ear. The rest of the disciples disappeared. One young man, probably Mark himself, ran away so fast he left his clothes behind. It was full-blown chaos.

And yet, Jesus did not flinch.

While everyone else was reacting, either by betraying, swinging, or running, Jesus stood steady. He didn't panic. He didn't try to escape. He didn't shame Judas or curse the soldiers. He called it like it was and surrendered to the Father's plan.

In that time, Jesus had more clarity than anyone else. He knew the cross was near, but He also knew this was not the end. He wasn't being overpowered. He was offering Himself on purpose. The others were driven by fear and confusion. Jesus moved with peace and purpose.

Peter still didn't get the mission. He wanted to fight the wrong enemy with the wrong weapon. Judas disguised betrayal with a kiss, offering fake intimacy while pushing Jesus toward pain. And Mark? He literally ran out of his own robe to avoid being identified. That detail isn't random. It shows what fear does when faith is only skin deep.

175

Notice the contrast: Judas brought a crowd armed with swords and clubs, as if Jesus were some dangerous criminal who needed to be subdued by force. But Jesus pointed out the absurdity of their approach. He had been teaching openly in the temple courts daily. They could have arrested Him anytime. Their nighttime raid with weapons revealed their own guilt and cowardice more than His supposed threat.

We all have moments where life unravels. A conversation goes sideways. Someone you trusted lets you down. Plans collapse. And your instinct is to freak out, fix it, or flee. But Jesus shows us a different way.

He didn't just endure the garden. He led through it. He stayed grounded because He trusted the bigger story. Scripture had already said this would happen. The Father had already prepared the path. Jesus knew who He was, and He refused to let the chaos around Him define His response.

The disciples' reactions show us different ways people respond to crisis: some betray, some fight back inappropriately, some flee entirely. But Jesus demonstrates the way of surrender without giving up, of peace without passivity. His calm wasn't denial or detachment; it was deep trust in God's sovereignty even when everything looked like it was falling apart.

CALL TO ACTION #1: Anchor your emotions to God's promises. Instead of reacting in panic, respond with prayer. Let Scripture stabilize your thoughts when fear takes over.

CALL TO ACTION #2: Stay present in pressure. Don't retreat or overreact. Breathe deep. Ask God to help you walk through, not run from, the hard moment.

Jesus did not flinch because He trusted what the Father already said. You can too.

77. The Cloud Rider
~Mark 14:53-65~

"I am," said Jesus, "and you will see the Son of Man seated at the right hand of Power and coming with the clouds of heaven."
Mark 14:62 (CSB)

THE greatest promises are made at the darkest hour. Jesus spoke His strongest words, not on a mountain but in a courtroom. His enemies surrounded Him, wanting Him dead, and He knew crucifixion was coming. But in that moment, Jesus said something that should radically change how every believer lives: "I'm coming back, and you will see me riding the clouds." That wasn't wishful thinking. That was a preview of coming attractions. Jesus looked those accusers in the eye and told them the story wasn't over. The One they were killing would return as the ultimate Victor. The Lamb they were sending to slaughter would come back as the Lion of Judah.

Coming with the clouds wasn't some clever poetry. That was Jesus claiming divine authority. In the Old Testament, God rides on clouds. He comes in clouds. He speaks through clouds. By using that imagery, Jesus was telling them exactly who He was and who He would always be. The beaten, mocked, and spat upon Savior will return as the triumphant King. Every knee that refuses to bow before Him will bow. Every tongue that curses His name will confess His lordship.

That promise changes everything about how we approach opposition. When people ridicule your faith, remember the Cloud Rider is coming. When your boss discriminates against you for your beliefs, remember the

Cloud Rider is coming. When culture tries to suppress biblical truth, remember the Cloud Rider is coming.

Jesus didn't promise you an easy road prior to His return. He promised a victorious ending. That's not the same thing, but it's infinitely better. Temporary struggle with eternal victory beats temporary comfort with eternal regret every single time.

The question isn't if Jesus will return. He promised He would and has never broken a promise. The question is if you're living like you believe it. Are you making decisions based on what's popular today or what will matter then? Are you building something that will last? The return of the Cloud Rider isn't just future hope; it's present power. It means you're never truly defeated, never permanently disadvantaged, never ultimately forsaken. The worst thing that happens to you in this life is not the last word. Jesus is.

Every trial you face is temporary. Every injustice you suffer has an expiration date. Every tear you cry will be wiped away. The Cloud Rider is coming, and when He does, everything broken will be made whole, everything wrong will be made right, and everyone who belongs to Him will be home.

CALL TO ACTION #1: Live like His return is imminent. Stop putting off the important conversations, the acts of service, the spiritual disciplines. If Jesus could return today, what would you wish you had prioritized?

CALL TO ACTION #2: Review your life through the lens of eternity. What are you building that will last beyond this world? What are you chasing that won't matter when the Cloud Rider returns?

78. I Swore I'd Never…
~Mark 14:66-72~

And Peter remembered when Jesus had spoken the word to him, "Before the rooster crows twice, you will deny me three times." And he broke down and wept. Mark 14:72

THE mirror doesn't lie, but sometimes you wish it would. The person staring back isn't who you thought you were. Somehow, without noticing, you've become someone you don't recognize. Your integrity feels fractured, your convictions compromised. This is Peter's moment in the courtyard, discovering that good intentions aren't enough when the pressure is real.

Just hours earlier, Peter was full of strong words. *"Even if everyone falls away, I will not" (Mark 14:29).* He drew a sword in the garden to fight for Jesus. He hung back at a distance after the arrest. He wanted to be brave, but there's no bravery in courage without surrender.

The pressure was real. By the fire, a servant girl recognized him and said, "You were with Jesus." Peter denied it. A few minutes later someone else said, "Hey, you're one of them too!" He denied it again. And then a third time, someone said his accent betrayed him. This time, Peter cursed and swore, *"I don't know this man you're talking about!" (Mark 14:71).*

The rooster crowed. And Peter remembered. That sound cut deeper than any sword could. The bravest of disciples had become a fearful bystander. The one who promised everything folded under pressure.

The text says *he broke down and wept.* Not a polite tear, but loud, heaving sobbing that only comes when failure feels final.

The courtyard was full of people who recognized Peter. He had a Galilean accent that stuck out in Jerusalem. His association with Jesus was well known. In those terrifying hours, Peter chose self-preservation over solidarity. He saved his skin but temporarily lost his soul.

This wasn't the end of Peter's story. It was a pivot point. Jesus didn't cancel Peter. He restored him. After the resurrection, Jesus reinstated Peter three times with affirmations of love to match his denials. Peter would go on to preach boldly at Pentecost and lead the church.

That's what grace does. Grace doesn't ignore failure. It transforms it. Grace doesn't pretend our mistakes don't matter but refuses to let them have the final word. Peter's denial was added to his testimony, evidence that God uses broken people to do big things.

Peter learned deeper faith, the kind that doesn't boast in strength but clings to mercy. He discovered that God isn't looking for flawless people; He's looking for honest ones. People who know they need help. People who fall down and get back up. People who stop pretending and start surrendering.

The man who denied Jesus three times would later face his own cross with courage. The disciple who ran in fear would die as a martyr. The difference wasn't that Peter became perfect; it's that he became dependent. He learned that divine strength shows up best in human weakness.

CALL TO ACTION #1: Rely on God's strength, not your own. Identify where you're trying to power through spiritual struggles alone. Ask for help and lean into community.

CALL TO ACTION #2: Accept God's restoration instead of living in shame. Stop rehearsing your worst moments. Let His grace rewrite the next chapter. Peter failed hard, but grace held firm and still does today.

79. Cancel The Noise
~Mark 15:1-5~

"Aren't you going to answer? Look how many things they are accusing you of!" But Jesus still did not answer, and so Pilate was amazed. Mark 15:1 (CSB)

YOU put on your noise canceling headphones and suddenly the world around you goes silent. The crying baby, jackhammer, office gossip all gets tuned out so you can focus on what really matters. Jesus had the ultimate pair, except His wasn't made in an electronics store; it was made by God. When the pressure and accusations came, He turned off human defense and tuned into God's silence.

Pilate was genuinely perplexed. The choice to not respond just wasn't in his criminal database. The religious leaders were throwing accusation after accusation and Jesus wasn't even trying to clear His name. Pilate kept pushing *"Aren't you going to answer? Look how many things they are accusing you of!"*

But Jesus had already decided what to tune into, and it wasn't the chatter of human opinion. His silence wasn't because He couldn't defend Himself; it was because He was on an entirely different channel. The lies they were throwing at Him were so ridiculous that to give them a response would be to give attention to liars. Hundreds of years earlier, Isaiah prophesied this exact moment. *He was oppressed and afflicted, yet he did not open his mouth. Like a lamb led to the slaughter and like a sheep silent before her shearers, he did not open his mouth (Isaiah 53:7).* Jesus wasn't winging it; He was on a divine mission.

Jesus knew something that Pilate didn't: the courts of earth aren't the final courts of appeal. While Pilate answered

181

to the justice system of Rome, Jesus only answered to the justice system of heaven. He didn't need Pilate's approval because He already had the Father's. He didn't need to defend His innocence because the only judge who mattered already knew the truth. This wasn't passive acceptance; this was active trust. Jesus filtered out the noise because He knew who He was and where this journey was going.

In the noisiest generation of human history, it's easy to feel overwhelmed by all the voices. Everyone has an opinion on everything all day long, and social media is the ultimate megaphone. Cancel culture, political rage, personal attacks, and accusations swirl all around us, but Jesus has the power to cancel all that noise. Sometimes the most powerful thing you can do is nothing at all.

CALL TO ACTION #1: Practice spiritual noise cancelling. What voices do you need to tune out this week? Toxic social media, gossip-filled conversations, or ungodly criticism that needs to be turned off? Choose silence over defensiveness.

CALL TO ACTION #2: Tune into heaven's frequency. When criticism or accusations come, ask yourself, "Am I responding from human systems or God's truth?" Let His opinion be more important than public opinion.

80. The Prisoner Exchange
~Mark 15:6-15~

At the festival Pilate used to release for the people a prisoner whom they requested. There was one named Barabbas, who was in prison with rebels who had committed murder during the rebellion.
Mark 15:6-7 (CSB)

YOU'RE sitting in a death row cell, counting down your final hours. You've exhausted all appeals. The governor has rejected your clemency petition. Tomorrow morning, you die for your crimes. Then footsteps echo down the corridor. The warden approaches with a look you've never seen before. "You're free to go," he says. "Someone else is taking your place." You'd think it was a cruel joke, except they're unlocking your cell and handing you street clothes.

That's what happened to Barabbas. He was guilty as a charged insurrectionist and murderer. Roman justice was about to be served with three nails and a cross. But then an innocent man stepped forward and volunteered to take his place. Barabbas walked out of prison while Jesus walked toward Golgotha.

Here's what makes this story stunning: Barabbas isn't just a historical figure. He's you. He's me. He's every person who has ever lived. We're all guilty before a holy God. Not of insurrection against Rome, but rebellion against heaven. We've all broken God's laws, chosen our way over His way, and earned the death penalty that sin demands.

Barabbas probably couldn't believe his luck. Free? Why? He'd done nothing to deserve clemency. That's the point. Grace isn't about what you deserve; it's about what someone else provides. Jesus didn't die because Barabbas was innocent. He died because Barabbas was guilty, and someone had to pay.

The crowd chose to free the criminal and crucify the Savior. Sounds backwards, but it was actually God's plan all along. Jesus came to take the place of every Barabbas. Every revel, every lawbreaker, every person who deserved punishment but received mercy instead.

What Barabbas did with his freedom, we don't know. But we know what we should do with ours. When someone takes your death sentence upon themselves, gratitude becomes a lifestyle. When you're pardoned from guilt you actually carried, worship becomes automatic. When you wake up free instead of dead, every day becomes a gift.

CALL TO ACTION #1: Accept your pardon. Stop trying to earn what Jesus already purchased. You were guilty; He made you free. Receive the grace that cost Him everything but costs you nothing.

CALL TO ACTION #2: Live like you've been pardoned. Let gratitude for your freedom fuel how you treat others. Show the same mercy you've received to someone who doesn't deserve it.

81. Mob Mentality
~Mark 15:16-20~

The soldiers led him away into the palace (that is, the governor's residence) and called the whole company together. They dressed him in a purple robe, twisted together a crown of thorns, and put it on him. And they began to salute him, "Hail, king of the Jews!"
Mark 15:16-18 (CSB)

MOB mentality is a dangerous thing. We see it in our own day with cancelled celebrities, viral hate threads, and protests that degenerate into riots. The herd instinct leads people to act out of character when they become caught up in the emotion or animosity of a crowd. The events of Mark 15 are one of the most dramatic examples of mass psychology gone terribly wrong. Roman soldiers, the religious elite, and the public lost themselves in something dark and cruel at Jesus' expense.

It began in the palace. Roman soldiers escorted Jesus inside, gathered the whole battalion, and decided to make a spectacle of His suffering. They dressed Him in a purple robe, placed a crown of thorns on His head, and mocked His identity. It wasn't duty. It was cruelty masquerading as humor. They hurled sarcastic insults, beat Him with a rod, and spat on Him. Empowered by the group, they stripped Him of His dignity.

Then the public joined in. As Jesus was crucified, people passed by, jeering and insulting Him. They quoted the words He had said in the past as if they discredited His mission. Religious leaders, people who should have been schooled in Scripture, joined the chorus. They said, *"He saved others, but he cannot save himself"* (Mark 15:31). But what they missed was chilling: Jesus had the power to come down from that cross, but He remained there to save them.

The sign above His head said, "King of the Jews." What was written as a mockery by Pilate was revealed as eternal truth. In their rage, the crowd wanted a show. But Jesus wasn't there to perform. He was there to redeem.

Crowd thinking can dull the conscience of the best people. From political mobs to trending outrage, our world can still echo the same energy found in Mark 15. When group emotion takes over, people often put aside their values. Compassion disappears. Truth gets distorted.

Jesus responded in restraint and mercy. Even while being tortured, He prayed for their forgiveness. He understood that the crowd didn't fully understand what they were doing. He was silent on that cross, resolute, and strong enough to endure humanity's worst to bring heaven's best.

CALL TO ACTION #1: Recognize the power of your individual influence. Remember that every crowd is made up of individuals making personal choices. Your decision to respond with kindness instead of cruelty and truth instead of mockery can influence others around you. Be the person who shifts the atmosphere from destructive to redemptive through your individual witness.

CALL TO ACTION #2: Be willing to stand apart. Stand for what is right when the crowd leans toward wrong. Speak with courage even when silence would be easier. Live in such a way that your faith shapes your choices more than public opinion. Let Jesus' courage shape yours.

82. Unloading Our Burdens
~Mark 15:20:32~

They forced a man coming in from the country, who was passing by, to carry Jesus's cross. He was Simon of Cyrene...
Mark 15:21 (CSB)

JESUS swayed under the burden of the rough wooden crossbeam. His flesh was already torn from hours of savage beating. Blood poured down His face from the crown of thorns pressed deeply into His scalp. His back was slashed open by the Roman scourge. Each stinging lash ripped flesh from His bones.

The soldiers suddenly realized He was in no condition to make it the rest of the way to Golgotha, so they forced a random passerby to carry the heavy wooden beam. Simon never volunteered to help. He wasn't looking for an opportunity to serve. Simon was just passing by, perhaps on his way home from working in the fields outside of Jerusalem. Roman soldiers grabbed him and thrust him into the most important moment in human history.

In that moment, Simon became the only person who literally shared Jesus' physical burden on the road to Calvary. While Simon shouldered the weight of the cross off of Jesus' shoulders, Jesus was getting ready to shoulder something infinitely heavier off the shoulders of all of humanity.

The burden Jesus would take upon His shoulders was far weightier than wood and iron nails. He was about to carry the full weight of sin, guilt, separation, and God's holy judgment that rightfully belonged to every person who had ever lived or would ever live. The man from Cyrene carried timber and metal. Jesus carried the sins of the world.

187

Simon's burden was temporary. It lasted only the distance from the Praetorium to Golgotha. Jesus' burden was eternal in scope. He took upon Himself every lie ever spoken, every heart ever broken by betrayal, every act of violence and cruelty, every moment of rage, jealousy, and hatred that had poisoned the human heart since the Garden of Eden. He bore the full weight of all human rebellion against God's holiness.

When Jesus hung on that cross, He wasn't simply dying a criminal's death alongside common thieves. He was being made sin itself so that He could take up the full weight of God's wrath and holy judgment that we deserved. The cross became the great exchange of all time. Our sin for His righteousness. Our condemnation for His complete forgiveness. Our spiritual death for His eternal life.

The stunning reality is that every burden you are carrying today that is the result of guilt, shame, regret, or wrong choices has already been carried by Jesus Christ. That crushing weight of "I'm not good enough" or "I've messed up too badly to be forgiven" has been carried to the cross and buried in His tomb. The nagging fear that God could never truly love someone with your past, your failures, your secret struggles? Jesus bore that burden in its entirety.

Just as Simon stepped in to carry Jesus' cross when He could no longer bear it alone, Jesus stepped in to carry our spiritual burdens when we could no longer bear them alone. The crucial difference is that Jesus didn't do it reluctantly like Simon initially did. He chose to do it willingly, voluntarily, out of perfect love for people who were still His enemies.

Your sins have been completely forgiven. Your guilt has been permanently removed. Your deepest shame has been replaced with honor as an adopted child of the living God. The exhausting burden of trying to earn God's approval through perfect behavior has been lifted forever. Jesus' perfect life is credited to your account.

This doesn't mean life becomes free of all burdens, trials, or difficulties. But it does mean you never again have to carry the crushing spiritual weight of condemnation before a holy God. When life feels overwhelming, when circumstances threaten to crush your spirit, when you're tempted to believe God is disappointed in you, remember the cross.

Remember clearly that Jesus has already carried the heaviest burden of your sin and shame, and declared with His final breath, "It is finished." The debt is completely paid. The burden is permanently lifted. You are forever free from condemnation.

CALL TO ACTION #1: Identify specific guilt and shame you're still carrying that Jesus has already resolved at the cross. Take time to confess these heavy burdens to Him honestly and receive His full forgiveness afresh today.

CALL TO ACTION #2: Like Simon carried Jesus' burden, find someone to support. Look for practical opportunities to help carry others' heavy burdens daily through acts of love, genuine encouragement, and consistently pointing them to Jesus' finished work on the cross.

83. Everything Is Changing
~Mark 15:33-41~

When it was noon, darkness came over the whole land until three in the afternoon. And at three Jesus cried out with a loud voice, "Eloi, Eloi, lemá sabachtháni?" which is translated, "My God, my God, why have you abandoned me?" Mark 15:33-34 (CSB)

THE world did not end that day, but it certainly felt like it. The sun disappeared at lunchtime. The ground trembled. A Roman crucifixion turned into a cosmic interruption. This was not just the death of a man; it was the unraveling of heaven's plan in real time.

Darkness swallowed the sky from noon until three. This was not a solar event or a cloudy day. Nature itself seemed to pause as the Light of the World was covered in the weight of sin. Creation responded to its Creator's agony with silence and shadows. The darkness was both literal and symbolic, representing the separation between God and humanity that sin had caused.

At the peak of that silence, Jesus cried out with gut-wrenching honesty. *"My God, my God, why have you abandoned me?" (Mark 15:34).* He was quoting Psalm 22, but this was not just recitation. It was the painful sound of perfect fellowship being torn. Jesus was not guilty, but He bore every sin as if He was. He felt what we often fear, that God had walked away.

This cry reveals the depth of what Jesus endured. For the first time in eternity, the Son experienced separation from the Father. The weight of humanity's rebellion, selfishness, pride, and hatred crashed down on Him. Every lie, every betrayal, every act of violence throughout history

190

found its way to the cross. Jesus didn't just die physically; He experienced spiritual death on our behalf.

Later, Jesus shouted again and breathed His last. This was not a whimper of defeat. It was a shout of completion.

Then something incredible happened. The curtain in the temple split from top to bottom. This curtain had separated the presence of God from the people. With it gone, God's presence was no longer restricted. The way was open.

Standing nearby, a Roman centurion watched it all. He had seen many men die, but never like this. Something about Jesus shook him to his core. He said, *"Truly this man was the Son of God" (Mark 15:39)*. In that confession, we hear the gospel beginning to spread beyond religious walls. A pagan soldier became one of the first to recognize Jesus' divine identity after His death.

The male disciples were gone, but the women stayed. Mary Magdalene, Mary the mother of James, and Salome remained at a distance. They did not run, hide, or forget. God honored their loyalty by allowing them to witness the most important moment in history. Their faithfulness positioned them to become the first witnesses of the resurrection just days later.

The cross changed everything: our access to God, our understanding of love, our hope for eternity. What looked like the end was actually the beginning of the greatest rescue mission ever accomplished.

CALL TO ACTION #1: Come boldly into God's presence today. Do not let guilt, fear, or your past keep you outside when Jesus has already opened the way in.

CALL TO ACTION #2: Tell someone what the cross means to you. Share personally and clearly how Jesus' death has changed your life forever.

84. Slow To The Party
~Mark 15:42-47~

Joseph of Arimathea, a prominent member of the Sanhedrin who was himself waiting for the kingdom of God, came and boldly went to Pilate and asked for Jesus' body. Mark 15:43 (CSB)

SOME people arrive early. Others take their time. And then there are those who wait until the very last moment but show up exactly when they are needed most. Joseph of Arimathea falls into that third category. This moment in Mark's Gospel happens after a dark and devastating day. Jesus has been crucified. His disciples have scattered. The city is settling down for the Sabbath. Most people assume the story is over. That is when Joseph steps forward.

A Risk Worth Taking

MARK calls attention to Joseph's social standing, making it clear that he was a *member of the Sanhedrin*, the Jewish ruling council that had earlier condemned Jesus. He had been part of the same institution that had voted to hand Jesus over to Pilate. Yet Joseph was not like the other Jewish leaders. He had been quietly waiting for the kingdom of God, watching and hoping, unsure when or how to act. Until now.

Courage comes in many forms. For Joseph, it came as a risky request. He went to Pilate, the Roman governor, and asked for Jesus' body. This was not a small favor. Crucified criminals were usually left on the cross as a warning to others. Claiming the body was a bold declaration of personal connection. Joseph made it clear to everyone watching that he was with Jesus.

The courage it took to make that request cannot be overstated. Pilate was no friend of the Jews, and the crowd had just minutes before demanded that Jesus be executed. Joseph's social standing, political influence, and personal safety were all on the line. Still, he acted. He could not undo what had been done, but he could give Jesus the honor He deserved.

The Power of Personal Sacrifice

RATHER than delegate, Joseph took responsibility. He bought linen cloth and personally wrapped Jesus' body. He laid Him in a tomb that had been cut out of rock—a tomb that was likely intended for Joseph himself. This act of generosity was not just practical; it was deeply symbolic. He gave Jesus the resting place of someone important, not the grave of a condemned man.

The irony is profound. The tomb Joseph offered was meant to be a place of final rest, yet it would only be used for three days. What Joseph believed was the end turned out to be the doorway to everything God had planned from the beginning. The grave did not keep Jesus. It simply held Him until the right time.

Joseph's decision was not spontaneous. He had likely followed Jesus quietly for some time, believing but unsure when to act. The cross changed that. Something about watching Jesus die removed the option of staying silent. Joseph chose to act when others had withdrawn. He stepped up when it mattered most.

Stepping Into Boldness

FAITHFULNESS sometimes means being slow to the party but arriving when the stakes are highest. Joseph reminds us that even delayed courage can be used by God. His moment of boldness, late as it seemed, played a part in setting the stage for resurrection.

CALL TO ACTION #1: Step out of hiding and represent Jesus publicly in your everyday life. If fear or reputation has held you back, ask God for boldness. Speak up in conversations where faith matters. Make it clear by your choices, relationships, and words that you follow Christ.

CALL TO ACTION #2: Leverage your influence, resources or opportunities to bring honor to Jesus. Like Joseph, you have something valuable to offer. Use your gifts, your position, or your possessions to serve God's purposes and care for others. Be willing to invest where it counts, even when it costs you comfort.

Joseph of Arimathea teaches us that it is not too late to act with courage. Even if you feel you have waited too long, God can still use your boldness to make a difference. Your next step of faith may be the one that helps prepare the way for resurrection in someone else's life.

85. Game Over
~Mark 16:1-8~

"Don't be alarmed," he told them. "You are looking for Jesus of Nazareth, who was crucified. He has risen! He is not here. See the place where they put him." Mark 16:6 (CSB)

EVERY great story needs a reversal. The moment when it looks like the hero has lost, but then everything shifts. Mark 16 describes that kind of moment for all of humanity. The death that seemed final wasn't. The tomb that should have stayed closed didn't. And the silence of Saturday gave way to the power of Sunday.

The Women Who Wouldn't Give Up

WHEN the Sabbath ended, Mary Magdalene, Mary the mother of James, and Salome brought spices to anoint Jesus' body. They weren't expecting a miracle. They were just trying to honor the One they loved. As they walked to the tomb early that morning, their conversation centered on a practical question: *"Who will roll away the stone for us?" (Mark 16:3)*. They had seen how large and heavy it was. They didn't have the strength to move it. Still, they showed up.

The Stone That Moved Itself

WHAT they found surprised them. The stone had already been moved. The entrance was open. But it wasn't opened for Jesus to get out; it was opened for witnesses to look in. Jesus had already risen. The obstacle they feared was already handled. God had gone ahead of them. The barrier that seemed immovable had been removed before they even arrived.

The Angel's Announcement

INSIDE the tomb, they saw a young man in white. His message was short but world-changing: *"He has risen! He is not here" (Mark 16:6).* Jesus, the one they watched die, was alive. That single statement flipped everything. The cross wasn't the conclusion. It was the setup. The tomb wasn't the final chapter. It was the turning point.

The Commission to Tell

THE angel didn't just deliver the news. He gave an assignment: *"Go, tell his disciples and Peter" (Mark 16:7).* Jesus wanted Peter, the one who had denied Him, to know he was still included. These women were the first to carry the good news. In a society that often overlooked them, God gave them the honor of telling the world that Jesus had risen.

The Empty Tomb That Filled the World

THE empty tomb means death does not get the final word. The resurrection confirms everything Jesus said. It proves that His sacrifice for sin was accepted and that eternal life is real.

CALL TO ACTION #1: Live as if the resurrection is real. Let it shape how you respond to fear, failure, and hardship.

CALL TO ACTION #2: Share the story with someone who needs hope. Start with what Jesus has done in your own life. The tomb is empty. The King is alive. The story is still going. Let that truth move you.

86. Go Time
~Mark 16:9-18~

He said to them, "Go into all the world and preach the gospel to all creation. Whoever believes and is baptized will be saved, but whoever does not believe will be condemned." Mark 16:15-16 (CSB)

THE last scene of every good movie always sets up the sequel. The hero has won the victory, but now the hard work really begins. Mark 16:9-18 is Jesus' last hoorah—His final instructions to His followers, marching orders that were good for that day, but are even more applicable for us today.

After the resurrection, Jesus appeared to individuals, but His followers had a hard time believing the reports. Mary Magdalene saw Jesus first, but when she reported to the disciples, *they did not believe it (Mark 16:11).* Two disciples saw Jesus on the road, but their reports were also disbelieved (Mark 16:13).

Even when Jesus finally appeared to the Eleven themselves, *He rebuked their unbelief and hardness of heart, because they did not believe those who saw after he had risen (Mark 16:14).* The resurrection was so unprecedented that even Jesus' closest followers had a hard time accepting it. This actually enhances the credibility of the resurrection accounts, since if the disciples had made the story up, they would not have included their own doubt and unbelief.

Once Jesus had convinced His disciples that He was truly alive, He gave them their marching orders: *"Go into all the world and preach the gospel to all creation."* This wasn't a suggestion, it was a command that would shape the mission of the church for the next 2,000 years.

197

The scope is breathtaking: all the world and all creation. Jesus wasn't just talking about Jerusalem or Judea. He was commissioning His followers to take the gospel to every nation, every people group, every corner of the earth.

This means going to the people we'd rather avoid, the neighbors who make us uncomfortable, the coworkers who seem hostile to faith, the family members who roll their eyes when we mention God, the communities that feel foreign to us, the places that require us to step way outside our comfort zones. Jesus is calling us to be gospel obsessed. Not comfortable, not selective, not strategic in a human sense, but absolutely consumed with getting this good news to everyone. Every single person matters to God, which means they should matter to us.

The message is equally clear: the good news that Jesus died for our sins and rose from the dead, offering forgiveness and eternal life to everyone who believes. Jesus made both a promise and a warning: *"Whoever believes and is baptized will be saved, but whoever does not believe will be condemned"* (Mark 16:16). The gospel is good news, but it demands a response. Belief isn't just intellectual assent; it's trust that leads to action. Those who truly believe will want to be baptized, publicly identifying themselves with Jesus. But those who reject the gospel face eternal condemnation.

After giving His final instructions, Jesus *was taken up into heaven and sat down at the right hand of God (Mark 16:19).* His earthly ministry was complete, but His heavenly ministry was just beginning. From His position of authority, Jesus continues to work through His followers. Mark concludes by noting that the disciples *went out and preached everywhere, while the Lord worked with them and confirmed the word by the accompanying signs (Mark 16:20).*

The Great Commission wasn't just a one-time command; it became the ongoing mission of the church. The Great Commission wasn't just for the original disciples, but for every follower of Jesus in every generation. The same command to go into all the world and preach the gospel applies to us today. We're called to be gripped by the good news, pushing past our preferences and comfort zones to reach people who desperately need to hear this life-changing news.

CALL TO ACTION #1: Take the Great Commission personally and find your role in fulfilling it. Evangelism isn't just for pastors and missionaries, but the responsibility of every believer. Identify the "world" God has placed you in—your workplace, neighborhood, school, or social circles. Ask God to show you specific people He wants you to reach with the gospel. Start by building genuine relationships, then look for opportunities to share your story of how Jesus has changed your life.

CALL TO ACTION #2: Mobilize your resources for global impact. The Great Commission requires the whole body of Christ working together. Pray regularly for missionaries and unreached people groups around the world. Give financially to support gospel work in places you can't personally go. Consider short-term mission trips or long-term missionary service if God is calling you to go. Use your skills, platform, and influence to advance the gospel wherever you are.

87. Divine Power, Human Grind
~Mark 16:19-20~

And they went out and preached everywhere, and the Lord worked with them and confirmed his word by the accompanying signs.
Mark 16:20 (CSB)

IMAGINE launching a startup with no funding, no connections, and a product that sounds too good to be true. Your founder just left the company, your target market thinks you're crazy, and the competition wants you shut down. This is the situation the early disciples faced when Jesus left them with the ultimate startup challenge: change the world.

But here's what made their impossible mission possible: they weren't going it alone. The followers of Jesus were tasked with a mission beyond imagination, one that would transform the world. Jesus commissioned His disciples to carry the gospel message to the ends of the earth and make disciples of all nations. It was a daunting charge.

The work of the church exploded after Jesus gave this life-changing commission and sent the Holy Spirit to power it forward. At the time of His Ascension, we read, *Jesus, after speaking to them, was taken up into heaven and sat down at the right hand of God (Mark 16:19).* The phrase *sat down* does not mean He is finished or resting. Instead, it means He took His rightful place in the highest position of the universe. As God's own Son, Jesus sat down as King, seated at the Father's right hand, from where He rules over all creation.

Jesus was not distant or removed, watching and waiting from a throne. He was the CEO of creation and would remain active in the mission of His kingdom, working intimately alongside His people. This reality set the disciples free and enabled them to face their task differently. Instead of struggling on their own with limited resources, the ultimate Partner had joined them.

Mark's final verse paints a picture of what the gospel does in people's lives. *And they went out and preached everywhere, and the Lord worked with them and confirmed the word by the accompanying signs (Mark 16:20)*. There is emphasis on work. The disciples worked hard, and the Lord worked with them. Divine human collaboration is at the center of the early church.

When heaven supports your grind, it changes everything. The disciples did their part; they brought passion, availability, and commitment. Jesus did His part; He brought power, authority, and supernatural confirmation. When human willingness meets divine ability, our efforts are transformed. Our courage is met with God's miracles. Our prayers are met with His healing. Our outreach is met with His transformation. In short, finite meets infinite, and the results defy expectations.

The phrase *confirmed the word by the accompanying signs* lets us know that Jesus was not going to leave His disciples to their own resources. Signs of His presence, healings, miracles, and supernatural interventions back up the message proclaimed by the early church. Jesus has not stopped confirming the message of the cross. The combination of human obedience and God's supernatural power will always result in confirmation and the advancement of His kingdom.

CALL TO ACTION #1: Recognize that you have a God-given assignment to get started. Identify the specific role where God wants to use you and take bold steps to step into that position.

CALL TO ACTION #2: Share your faith boldly and expect God to confirm His word through your life.

Wrapping Up

Wrapping Up the Remarkable Journey of Jesus... and You

AS we close out this journey through Mark's Gospel, take a moment to look back. What began with a bold announcement—*The beginning of the gospel of Jesus Christ, the Son of God*—has unfolded into the most breathtaking story in human history.

You've walked with Jesus as He healed the broken, silenced storms, raised the dead, confronted corruption, and gave His life as a ransom for many. You've witnessed a Savior who doesn't play by the rules of religion or social norms. His authority is unmatched. His compassion is deep. His mission is unstoppable.

From chapter 1 to chapter 16, Mark shows us a Jesus who is remarkably present, remarkably powerful, and remarkably personal. And now, the story is in your hands.

This Isn't the End

MARK'S Gospel ends abruptly. The resurrection happens, the tomb is empty—and then the women flee, trembling and amazed. No tidy wrap-up. No grand summary. Why? Because the story isn't finished.

Mark's Gospel was always meant to be more than a record of what Jesus did. It's a call to step into what Jesus is still doing. You're not just a reader of the story, you're a continuation of it.

Jesus didn't come just to be admired. He came to be followed. The same Jesus who called fishermen to leave their nets and follow Him is still calling. The same Jesus who saw the overlooked, touched the untouchable, and forgave the unforgivable is still moving. And He's inviting you to be part of what He's doing today.

A Faith That Moves

THIS journey through the second Gospel wasn't meant to give you head knowledge; it was meant to stir heart transformation. A faith that merely observes Jesus is not the kind of faith He calls us to. He's looking for people who respond. Who take the next step. Who live with the boldness of those who know the King is alive and the kingdom is near.

Every healing, every teaching, every confrontation in this Gospel was a preview of the kingdom Jesus is building, a kingdom that looks nothing like the empires of this world. It's a kingdom marked by love, humility, justice, grace, and courage. And now, you're called to represent that kingdom.

What does that look like? It looks like choosing character when shortcuts are easier. Speaking truth when silence feels safer. Loving the hard-to-love. Giving when it costs. Forgiving when it hurts. Trusting when you don't understand. Worshiping when you don't feel like it. Showing up when you'd rather withdraw.

It's a remarkable life—not because it's perfect, but because it's built on the unshakable foundation of a Savior who still reigns.

When the Gospel Gets Personal

IF the Gospel of Mark has done its job, then you haven't just learned more about Jesus; you've met Him. You've seen how He interrupts ordinary moments with extraordinary grace. You've seen how He handles storms, shame, betrayal, fear, and even death. Now it's your turn.

What would it look like to let Jesus shape how you handle conflict? How you scroll? How you talk to your friends? How you treat your family? How you face anxiety?

Jesus isn't confined to the pages of this Gospel. He wants to speak into your everyday life. He wants to rewrite your story. And He invites you to live in a way that reflects His goodness to a world that desperately needs something real.

Keep Going

THE Gospel isn't a class you finish; it's a life you live. Mark may be the shortest Gospel, but it leaves a long-lasting impact because it points us to a Jesus who is still writing stories today...through people like you.

Wherever you go from here, carry this truth with you: Jesus is still moving. He's still healing. He's still calling. And He's still building His Church, one transformed life at a time.

So keep reading. Keep praying. Keep following. Let the wonder of Jesus never grow stale. Let the truth of His resurrection continue to shape your identity, your decisions, your dreams, and your direction.

Because the Son of God didn't just do remarkable things; He makes people remarkable by His grace.

Final Thought

YOU don't need to be famous, flawless, or fearless to be part of this story. You just need to say yes. Yes to Jesus. Yes to growth. Yes to walking by faith. Yes to the remarkable journey that continues when you close this book.

Let's go.

TOPICAL INDEX
Sorted By Chapter

FOR MORE RESOURCES FROM RYAN HELLER GO TO

SERMONSIDEKICK.COM
RYANHELLER.ORG

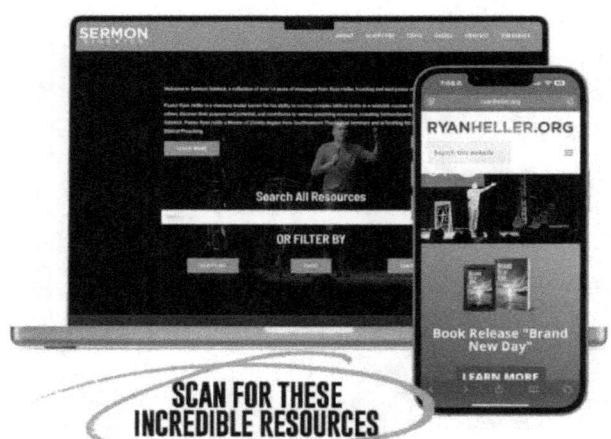

SCAN FOR THESE INCREDIBLE RESOURCES